HOW WE DESIRE

CAROLIN EMCKE was born in 1967. She studied philosophy, politics and history in London, Frankfurt and at Harvard. From 1998 to 2013 she reported from war and crisis zones including Kosovo, Afghanistan, Pakistan, Iraq, Gaza and Haiti. She has written a number of books and in 2016 she received the Peace Prize of the German Book Trade, which has also been won by Svetlana Alexievich, Orhan Pamuk and Susan Sontag.
carolin-emcke.de
@C_Emcke

IMOGEN TAYLOR is based in Berlin. She is the translator of Sascha Arango, Dirk Kurbjuweit and Melanie Raabe, among others.

HOW
WE
DESIRE

CAROLIN EMCKE
TRANSLATED FROM THE GERMAN
BY IMOGEN TAYLOR

TEXT PUBLISHING MELBOURNE AUSTRALIA

textpublishing.com.au

The Text Publishing Company
Swann House
22 William Street
Melbourne Victoria 3000
Australia

Originally published as *Wie wir begehren* © S. Fischer Verlag GmbH, Frankfurt am Main, 2012
This edition published by The Text Publishing Company, 2018

Cover design by W. H. Chong
Page design by Jessica Horrocks
Typeset by J&M Typesetting

Printed and bound in Australia by Griffin Press, an accredited ISO/NZS 14001:2004 Environmental Management System printer

ISBN: 9781925603613 (paperback)
ISBN: 9781925626650 (ebook)

A catalogue record for this book is available from the National Library of Australia

AUTHOR'S NOTE

Names and other identifying details have been
changed to protect the privacy of individuals.

'Et se trouve autant de différence de nous
à nous-mêmes que de nous à autrui.'

*(And there is as much difference between
us and ourselves as between us and others.)*

MONTAIGNE

—

'Die Saite des Schweigens gespannt
auf die Welle von Blut…'

*(The string of silence drawn taut
over the swell of blood…)*

INGEBORG BACHMANN

I was having such trouble with the world
that I began to make up proverbs.
There are long truths and short truths.
And if punishment doesn't swiftly follow,
you must live away your guilt through life.

JAN SKÁCEL

Perhaps that is the reason for this story. Perhaps it has to begin with guilt—with a guilt that cannot be chipped away at, but has to be lived away through life. Perhaps it is an illusion that guilt can be hammered away at, as if it were ore or coal, as if you could knock chunks out of it—little lumps that can be carried off or crumbled to a powder or dissolved. Perhaps telling stories belongs to life the way silence belongs to death. And perhaps the only way to grasp the long truth of this story is to tell it.

I don't know why we were singled out. The other children, and in particular the boys, stood around us, taunting. Maybe there were only boys apart from me; I wouldn't have noticed; the differences didn't much matter at that time—not to me, at any rate. They hung around like a pack of wolves, in a shapeless circle with no apparent order. Awkward but viciously determined, one or other of them would venture forward now and then and give Daniel or me a shove to the shoulder: 'Go on!'

We were standing at the edge of the muddy football pitch that was not in fact a real football pitch, but only a large clearing on the wooded hill next to the school. I don't suppose you get that any more—an unpaved playground. This place was a semi-wilderness beside the schoolyard proper with its benches and railings and the perpetually draughty grey toilet block. There were two goals without nets and a pitch without markings.

'Go on!' They were awed by their own courage, afraid of their own cowardice and intently aware of what the others might think of them. 'Go on, fight.' They swooped and then backed away, their eyes on each other, their diminutive bodies leaning forwards slightly, their heads low—a little too aggressive, a little too submissive, on their guard lest the violence they were trying to direct at us might turn against them—a mob of children.

It was our first day of secondary school. The day had begun in the gym; I don't know why the assembly to welcome the new arrivals and announce the first-year class teachers wasn't held in the school hall. We sat on wooden benches next to our mothers and fathers, waiting to see which of the three classes we'd been assigned to. It was soon clear what we could expect from the teachers and whether or not they were popular; we had only to listen to the applause—or lack of it—given by the older students who were attending the ceremony out of boredom or spite. Thinking about it today, I realise how awful those three teachers must have felt. As they stood there at the end of the gym under the basketball hoop, their names were greeted with loud whistles or a mere spattering of applause, so that they knew the second they were appointed class teachers that they'd lost all authority in the eyes of their new pupils. I suppose that's why the older students were there—because it was their only opportunity all year for revenge. I remember feeling a little sorry for those defenceless teachers. And I remember that although I couldn't have put a name to it at the time, the atmosphere of collective judgement gave me the creeps.

Next we listened to the alphabetical lists, waiting for the first letters of our surnames, hearing our names read out and wondering anxiously whether our primary-school friends would also be announced. I was lucky. My best mates of the past few years were all put in the same class as me. It didn't matter who the unknown children were whose names followed; just as long as you avoided being pushed into that new world alone. Then the assembly was over. Our parents left and we got into our new groups and followed our new teachers down the stairs to the lower-school building. It was a little out of the way, at the foot of the hill; we were in our own sunken world, no longer quite primary school, but not yet properly secondary school either.

And now here we were, at the corner of the football pitch, next to the nettle-covered slope. It was one of the first breaks and must have been a short one because the long break was always used to play football. The short breaks weren't good for anything much. Down here by the lower-school buildings there was no baker's, no ice-cream shop, nowhere you could have slipped off to. Later there would be the smokers' corner but we were too young for that—or too unadventurous. Perhaps we simply had too little imagination to know how to express our love of transgression.

We didn't want to—neither Daniel nor I. Rather furtively, we exchanged glances; we didn't know each other. I had no idea what primary school Daniel had been to, but I knew I'd never seen him before. He had blond hair and far-apart green eyes, and he was a little taller than me, though not much. His shoulders were square, his arms slightly too long. But I won't have noticed that at the time; we all had something too long or too short; we were all slightly out of joint, if only because we thought the others might think we were. Daniel was pleasant looking. There was no reason why he should have been singled out like that on our first day of school. It was arbitrary. It just happened to be us.

I didn't really know what it was all about—why we were supposed to fight. Daniel hadn't done anything to me; there was no motive. I'd often got into scuffles. I'd had a fight with someone on my first day of kindergarten, and again on my first day of primary school, so in principle there was no reason not to get into a fight on my first day at secondary school. I had an older brother; fighting was part of my everyday repertoire of survival. But I had to be angry about something; I had to be convinced that the other person had done something mean. I couldn't lash out at somebody just like that, without being provoked. Or maybe I just didn't get the game—this attempt by an amorphous group to establish a hierarchy, this desperate attempt on the part of each individual pupil to keep out of the circle, avoid being put to the test, avoid being ostracised on that first day. That was the only reason they formed the circle, the only reason they dared go so far—they had no confidence in themselves. That was the only reason they needed these situations that allowed them to label others as weaklings.

The trouble was that both could be deemed a weakness—fighting and not fighting. If you let the others egg you on, it might mean that you didn't dare stand up to the group. If you refused, it might mean that you doubted your own ability to win a fight. One would be a psychological defeat, the other physical. I admit that, as an experienced little sister, I wasn't remotely bothered by the prospect of losing. I was used to losing. All through my childhood, I lost every test of strength, every athletic challenge, every fight. I can't recall regarding the individual challenges as particular losses, even if they added up to a long string of defeats. Was I stirred by athletic ambition to give it a go—or did I stand my ground out of pride? I can't say. I was probably just stubborn.

When I ask myself why I wasn't afraid of losing back then, on my first day of school, I can only suppose it had something to do with the fact that I always lost anyway. I don't think I even stopped to wonder. Maybe that was the best protection I could have had—my fearlessness.

The incident ended as suddenly and wordlessly as it had begun—because the bell rang for the end of break, or because a teacher appeared. Everyone scattered. The tension evaporated. By the next day, most of the children seemed to have forgotten that they'd tried to get us to fight. That was my first encounter with Daniel.

—

I don't know why he took his life. I've never asked anyone—only myself. I wasn't surprised, although that's the usual reaction; someone dies by his own hand and we express surprise. Of course it was a shock when years later—years after that first day of school and some time after Daniel had left our school—I was told: 'Daniel's dead.' I wasn't even eighteen at the time. *Daniel's dead.* It sounded shabby. Even as I heard the words, I felt disgust at them. They were words I would hear more than once and they invariably conveyed more than shock; there was always something else, beneath the stunned tones. When I first heard people talking about Daniel's suicide, I thought I detected in their tones of shock the universal desire for scandal, the voyeuristic love of sensation that allows people to turn another person's demise into a celebration of their own survival. But there was something else too. *Daniel's dead*—the words were also a kind of corroboration. The more appalled the voices that remarked on his suicide, the more satisfied they sounded. It was as if Daniel's death were a late triumph—as if the hunt had come to a successful end, the weakling been identified after all.

Of course I wondered why he had taken his life. I wanted to know whether there had been a letter, some form of announcement or explanation—whether he'd left anything behind. But if I wondered why Daniel had committed suicide, it wasn't because I *couldn't* come up with any reasons, but because I *could*—and because I wanted to know whether the reasons I'd come up with were the same as his. I wanted to know how much his death had to do with us—how much it had to do with all those circles that were drawn, circles that included and excluded and didn't always break up as quickly as that first circle on the football pitch. What was it about him that prevented him from surviving? Was there even anything about him? What went wrong in his life? Was there a line he couldn't cross—a line that might have protected him? Had we drawn such a line? Did his death have anything to do with him—or with us—at all? Did it have anything to do with the world in which he lived? Why him and not me? Weren't there just as many reasons why it could have been me? Why had I emerged from that time unscathed? I'd been in that circle with him. Couldn't it just as easily have been me? Isn't it arbitrary? Is there any way of telling who will emerge unscathed from those years of uncertainty, that childhood that is no longer childhood?

Was the reason I didn't discover my desire until years after I'd left school the same reason why Daniel took his life? Was the longing that we couldn't understand back then, couldn't discover, couldn't live, the same longing?

—

The list was neat and tidy. The lines were all dead straight. The right angle where the two axes crossed had been

8

drawn with a set square. It looked like a piece of homework set by one of our teachers, as if our teachers monitored us even in areas that didn't fall under their jurisdiction. The names had been entered meticulously into the table. There were two lists. On the boys' list, the boys' names ran from top to bottom and the girls' names from left to right. On the girls' list, it was the other way round.

The world divided, splitting into two sexes even before our bodies had become aware of the divide—before they had properly discovered that they belonged to one sex or the other. Certainly, that rift in the world had been there before, a natural law with nothing natural about it. But it hadn't really mattered. There were boys and girls, brothers and sisters. Of course we had looked at each other and shown ourselves to each other, fully aware of our differences. Hadn't I, barely four years old, surrendered a treasured Smurf to the boy next door to bribe him to slide his foreskin up and down for me? It's true, I could have got my brother to show me, but I don't think he'd have let me have it so cheap. Of course those subtle differences already existed. Until now, though, they had only rarely *made a difference*.

There were separate changing rooms for PE and we vanished into them for a few minutes at the beginning of every lesson—rooms so gloomy and musty that we would associate sexuality with darkness and sweat right from the start. We left our shared life, splitting in half, as it were, for that brief moment of nudity, to come together again, dressed, only minutes later. At the end of the lesson we returned to slip back into our clothes. I can't recall anyone ever using the mildewed showers in the changing rooms. Our timetable didn't allow for showers; it wasn't part of the plan that students should wash their sweaty bodies. PE finished just before break and we barely had time to change before the next lesson began over in the other building. A long shower—let alone make-up— was impossible. It seemed not to have occurred to the teachers or school management that teenagers had bodies they might want to wash. On the one hand, then, they regarded us as too young to be sufficiently aware of our bodies to care whether or not they were clean and fresh-smelling. On the other hand, they regarded us as too old to undress in front of each other. Togetherness and homogeneity were not to be. Sexual dualism and hetero-sexuality were givens, even before gender or sexuality had properly matured.

About fifteen years later, I met a hermaphrodite for the first time. Until then, I hadn't realised there was such a thing. For me, hermaphrodites were divine figures from Greek mythology, conflated beings, half male, half female. That was as much as I knew. I'd just split up from my boyfriend and was on holiday with a mate from university, staying with friends.

One afternoon when we were getting drunk and

playing Trivial Pursuit, a couple dropped in on our hosts—an Italian photographer and his girlfriend Nicola. She was young, pretty, slim and elegant, and cheerfully joined in that absurd game. There was nothing remarkable about her except that she was strikingly incapable of answering even the most straightforward questions. This can, of course, happen to anyone playing Trivial Pursuit; the game is not designed to reward a classical education, and even the most encyclopaedically educated can come to grief when asked what Fred Flintstone's mother-in-law is called or who was running next to Jürgen Hingsen when he was disqualified. From that point of view, there was nothing unusual in having to pass. But not only did Nicola seem unable to answer the questions; she didn't even seem able to put them in any kind of context. It wasn't her lack of knowledge that was disconcerting, but her apparent lack of an associative network that might have allowed her to link up individual topics—her lack of a stratified system of knowledge. Nicola seemed to have flowers of knowledge floating, apparently unconnected, on a watery surface, blown here and there by the wind, unrooted.

She was by no means upset by the way the game was going; she didn't even seem to notice that there were different kinds of questions—straightforward questions and trickier ones, questions that tested the peripheries of knowledge and others that covered more familiar areas.

She laughed at her cluelessness and at ours, and she drew card after card, always with the hope that this time she'd be able to get the right answer. She fished the water with a wide-meshed net and was delighted at each rare flower that was caught in it. Her lack of concern at her own ignorance was infectious and liberating, and so we laughed and drank and played, and wondered only slightly at this charming woman.

A little later, some of the party went to the beach to swim. I stayed behind and began to cook, washing courgettes and aubergines, chopping them in half lengthways, then slowly peeling cloves of garlic and cutting them into thin slices. I don't know why I remember everything so clearly. I went out to the terrace to pick some oregano from the herb planter and suddenly my friend was standing next to me saying: 'There's something not right.' She didn't say: 'There's something not right *about her*', and yet it was immediately clear whom she meant. When they'd been swimming it had become evident that the beautiful young woman had male genitals. For the rest of that evening nobody mentioned what was on everyone's mind—not until Nicola and her boyfriend had left. Then our hosts told us what they knew about Nicola.

Nicola had a body that couldn't be unequivocally classified as one sex or the other. She wasn't transsexual; she hadn't had sex reassignment surgery. She was intersexual. She hadn't been born into a body whose sex she was uncomfortable with; she had been born into a body that had developed two sexes—that was, as it were, undecided. Puberty, when her breasts developed at the same time as her penis, was for her a time of continuous ostracism, because her ambivalent gender was perceived, more than anything, as a social threat. One of the most distressing experiences of her school years was, hardly surprisingly, connected with the changing rooms—places of norm-reinforcement from which she was excluded because they demanded unambiguity. In the end she stopped going to school—not because she wasn't capable of meeting the academic requirements or because she didn't want to learn, but because there was no place for her in that divided world. That was the reason for the gaps in her knowledge.

Nicola brought home to us something that applied just as much to us as it did to her—that sexuality is prescribed by norms. We are expected to consider such a prescription as natural and we accept it unquestioningly, because for us, in our bodies, it's no trouble to do so. We slip into norms the way we slip into clothes, putting them on because they're laid out ready for us, because someone pulls them over our heads, because they come to fit us or because, without even noticing, we come to fit them. We only notice norms as norms if we don't comply with them, don't fit them—whether or not we want to. Anyone with white skin regards the category of skin colour as irrelevant because in the life of a white person in the West, skin colour *is* irrelevant. Anyone who is heterosexual regards the category of sexual orientation as irrelevant because in the life of a heterosexual, sexual orientation *can* be irrelevant. Anyone who feels comfortable in his or her body regards the category of sex as self-evident because his or her body is never questioned.

Anyone who complies with the norms can afford to doubt their existence.

Particularly strange was the boy-girl division at the outdoor pool belonging to our school, where we were made to swim every year, long before it was anywhere near warm or sunny. I seem to recall that there were neither lockers nor benches where we could leave our things. In fact, there was nothing apart from this separation into girls and boys. Not that it stopped me from swimming in bathing trunks. As long as I had nothing I could have covered with a swimsuit, I saw no reason to wear one. I saw no sense in a swimsuit as a mere marker of female identity, and nor, I am glad to say, did my mother. It wasn't even a conscious act of rebellion. I had no aversion to embodying anything girlish; it was just that I barely did. So why bother with a swimsuit? I'd probably have disliked it just as much the other way round—if we children had all worn swimsuits to begin with and then, at a certain age, half of us had been expected to switch to swimming trunks. I'd probably have wanted to avoid that too—being marked out from the others, suddenly having to be different from what had previously been regarded as normal.

What would it have been like, I wonder, if the divide hadn't existed? If the differences had been considered of no consequence? If the categories 'boys' and 'girls' had been irrelevant? If sex had been classed like hair colour—as a trait, a physical attribute that varied without social consequences, without collective pigeonholing? And what if the table of names hadn't been divided into girls and boys, but had simply listed all the pupils, regardless of sex? Such a thing hadn't even entered our minds—that boys could like boys and girls girls.

The table did the rounds. We passed it from desk to desk, filling in the rows next to our names, arms crooked around the paper to stop our neighbours from looking—as if they wouldn't be seeing it all a few minutes later anyway—and in the box below each boy's name we entered a mark: 2, 3-, 5, 1- or 4+. We didn't declare our likes and dislikes in direct conversations or secret love letters, but in this list that was handed around the entire class, and we gave marks to express our feelings—or what we took for feelings—as if completing a record of achievement. We had no other language. And so we entered these figures into the table, doling out numbers and verdicts to everybody in class—everybody of the opposite sex, at least—even the ones we didn't actually feel anything for, like or dislike. Those we gave a 3- or a 3+, some mediocre mark that meant nothing. And we were ruthless about giving bad marks to anyone we found strange or weird, anyone who aroused annoyance or disgust in us—emotions we had no outlet for other than this list. None of us stopped to worry that those pupils might feel disappointed or hurt.

How did it start? Who came up with this appalling idea? Was it someone in our class—or had we simply inherited a custom that was passed down from year to year? Were we citing a tradition without recognising it as such, the way you rake leaves in the autumn and burn them, only because the season seems to dictate it?

It was horrific. Knowing full well that the whole class got to see the list, we would discover that the boy we liked couldn't stand us, or—as bad, if not worse—that the boy we liked was liked just as much by all the other girls, or... The possibilities for humiliation and pain were endless. The list was passed along the rows and everyone was witness to his or her popularity, or lack of it. These days, Facebook has replaced such homemade public arenas, but the visible nature of the potential hurt hasn't changed. Why did we do it?

Daniel and I were lucky. We got off scot-free on those lists. We were always at the top end of the range, always got good marks and were able to concentrate on whether or not those marks had come from the pupils we wanted them from.

The lists were passed about for a while. New copies were made and new marks given—and then one day, when all the good marks and all the bad marks had gone to the same names for goodness knows how many lists in a row, the tables were shortened. I don't know whose idea it was. As if the less popular no longer counted—as if they were superfluous or so hopelessly unpopular with everyone that there was no point even in rating them, or as if they no longer belonged—they were excluded, dropped off the list. New lists were drawn up, and again there was one for the boys where the boys' names were on the vertical axis and the girls' names on the horizontal axis, and another one, the other way round, for the girls. But this time there were only six boys' names and six girls' names. The two lists were now so short that both tables fitted on one piece of paper.

The rest no longer figured.

⸺

My first boyfriend was called Ben. He had dark curly hair and an easygoing, slightly shuffling gait. It wasn't altogether clear why Ben was my first boyfriend. It had come about through the lists: I liked him, and we had reached an age when you were supposed to have a friend and when friendship was supposed to be different from the way it used to be. It was more decision than desire. Maybe it was just that secondary school was perceived as another world and because, being in 'observation grade', as it is known in some parts of Germany, we first-year pupils may not have felt particularly observed, but we did want to observe ourselves.

In those first years of secondary school, everything went on at once—children's games and teenage rituals. We'd play for hours on the slippery stones by the river, squatting on them at high tide and waiting for the wash from passing container ships to catch us, and playing ducks and drakes at low tide, if the water was calm, with the flattest pebbles we could find. Down by the river, time was something you could see; you only had to look at the lines on the shore separating dark from light and wet from dry—or at the wreck of a ship run aground, almost completely submerged at high tide, but sticking right out of the water at low tide, so that you could see the top third of its hull. Even when the tide was out, though, it was too far to reach on foot. It stood there, forbidding and un-get-at-able, and only in winter, if the river froze and the ice floes were conveniently positioned, could you risk the walk to that mysterious ship, listening closely to every creak to make sure the ice wasn't cracking underfoot.

We plunged into the woods, crawling into foxes' dens in the bracken, or building tree houses in the copper beeches that seemed to have been made for climbing. Apart from the occasional dog owner, we had the woods almost to ourselves. We'd disappear when school finished at midday, sometimes taking Ryvita sandwiches to keep us going, and we wouldn't re-emerge until the evening, filthy and almost always covered in grazes.

But we hadn't quite found the right rhythm. Or maybe it was only me. Looking back, I have the impression I was always too early or too late—never in step with time. I had missed the moment when it was no longer the done thing to disappear into the woods or roam around by the river. The woods were my world, an inexhaustible domain of wild berry bushes and dried-up stream beds, smells and sounds, plants and trees, providing clues and promising intelligence to anyone who knew how to read the signs.

The idea was all my own. I whispered it into my dog's ear, but let no one else in on my plan. I wanted to get to know every inch of the woods behind my parents' house, to scout out its narrow, overgrown paths, to explore the insides of the rhododendrons with their gnarled twigs— bend back the branches very slowly, without breaking them, and then plunge into the deep, spherical plants that looked so impenetrable on the outside, with their dark-green roofs, and were always so airy and spacious on the inside.

I wanted to learn how to tell trees apart just from the feel of them. I would close my eyes, lay my hands on the bark of the trees I knew and slowly touch their skin, running my fingertips along the grooves, feeling my way up and down them, discovering rough gristly ridges like wooden veins and trying to impress on myself: that was the skin of an oak, dry as a handshake. I continued the exercise: this smooth skin with the slightly grainy dust that rained down when you rubbed your hands over the trunk, its bark so taut you'd think something were trying to force its way out, perhaps a new shoot about to erupt right beneath your hands—that was the skin of a beech.

There was one particular beech in the woods, which grew beneath the path. Whenever it rained, the crevice where the branches met the trunk filled a little with water. It felt like an armpit, except that the dip faced upward so that the rain could gather there. When I patted the inside of this armpit, my dog would jump up at the tree and drink the water from the wooden hollow.

Then there were the trees with parchment skin— their thin trunks slender and boy-like, their papery bark flaking off in places like scabs. These were birches, ashy trees that I would later come to associate with Bergen-Belsen, after being taken to the former concentration camp on a cold foggy spring day by my father who had decided that we ought to see it, although we were only children. All those milky-coloured birches by the mass graves had disturbed me. It probably wasn't so much the colour that troubled me as the fact that they were growing there at all—growing out of *that* earth, rather than withering and shrivelling up and perishing.

Over time, I grew more and more familiar with the woods, and I set to work on the smells next, breaking off twigs and plucking flowers to sniff at them, stirring up damp leaves or peeling flat cakes of peat off stones and burying my nose in them. I set up archives in my head to chart that brief moment, perhaps the last half hour, before a downpour, and the first few minutes after the rain's stopped, when it has soaked the woods and everything smells different—the wet, steaming stones, the bushes, the grass. I stashed away what I had observed of these transformations—the way nature opens up and stretches and flexes, exposing itself and turning inside out. The way it can change consistency to grow softer, wetter, smoother and more porous—or drier, more brittle, more gnarled. The way it can contract or grow bigger—a living, breathing being that speaks many languages.

And so it seemed to me the most natural thing in the world to go to the den in the woods for my first kiss. Others' stories of their first kisses always sound so romantic, so magical. The most exciting thing about my first kiss was that it was the first. We'd often been to the den in the woods; it was our private place that belonged to us alone. We had built the hiding place ourselves, out of a fir trunk that lay crosswise, surrounded by beeches and ash trees. The fir had fallen in such a way that part of the trunk lay suspended above the forest floor. Interwoven with branches we had gathered, it was like a little wooden igloo. That's where we kissed, and the slightly metallic taste of Ben's mouth mingled with the smell of fresh warm leaves.

On a class trip, not long after, Ben came to my room one evening and knocked. When I opened the door, he sang 'All My Loving' to me. Ben liked the Beatles; he knew all their songs off by heart. And he clearly liked me. I sat on the edge of the lower bunk and listened, not knowing why I felt so strange. I looked back and forth between Ben, standing there in a semicircle of boys from our class, who had clearly dared him, and the girls in my room, who envied me something that seemed to me faintly embarrassing rather than enviable.

I don't know whether that was the moment I stopped liking Ben. He had sung beautifully, and everyone else had taken it as proof of how much in love he was. But I couldn't forget the public nature of the serenade—the open door, the boys standing behind him, almost wetting themselves with excitement (would he really do it?), overawed by this mate of theirs who'd pulled off something they'd never manage—because they didn't know any songs off by heart, or didn't have anyone to sing to. And I couldn't help thinking that the semicircle of boys around him was a little like that circle on our first day. Ben stood at a slight angle, turned half to me, half to the boys, as if to keep an eye on them, as if he didn't dare turn away from them altogether. Perhaps that's unfair. Perhaps he was only seeking a little reassurance, keeping his stage fright at bay. Perhaps it was only natural. But however nicely Ben sang and however much I liked him, it was clear to me even then that he'd sung for the boys.

—

What am I looking for? Daniel is dead. He took his life, like so many other young people. Back then, school suicide was a quiet, solitary affair, without witnesses. No big exits, no internet announcements, no black combat gear or camouflage masks, no semi-automatics from Dad's weapon arsenal. Back then, school children committed suicide without trying to drag others to their deaths with them; they killed themselves out of hopelessness, despair and desperation, without drawing on revenge fantasies or on fantasies of omnipotence or destruction.

No re-enacted executions, no carefully choreographed performances that claim uniqueness while imitating virtual characters, and hope to garner attention at last in an unforgettable act of killing, but instead condemn themselves to oblivion by using gestures and masks that are mere quotations from the history of cinema or gaming. Who remembers the faces of the Columbine or Winnenden killers? Who remembers their names? They are forgotten. If anything is remembered, it's the video games that provided the aesthetic models—games that were emulated for one day—one death.

Daniel took his life. I don't know whether he left a letter. I expect that everyone who loses a beloved person to suicide looks for—hopes for—a farewell letter, words to release them from their helplessness, if only so that they have an answer to give when people ask for reasons.

My grandfather took his life. I didn't know until I was in my early twenties. He was a melancholic; I suppose that's what people said in the sixties, before depression was a socially accepted illness. It's nothing to be ashamed of. My grandfather had lived a rich and intense life consciously and appreciatively. He left a letter, but maybe it wasn't even necessary to say goodbye. He had lived facing life. Maybe he was able to die facing death. Maybe he had to die facing death. Maybe anything else would have weakened his resolve.

It's like Orpheus and Eurydice. On his way back from Hades into the world of the living, Orpheus can only hold Eurydice's hand; he mustn't look back at her, because a glance at her, his loved one, would be a glance back into the realm of the dead that he is leading her out of. But to look away from hope like that is impossible to lovers, who seek the openness of love and life.

How sweet, o gods, the hope
You've sent me from on high,

But with that hope comes pain
That tells me I must die.[1]

Maybe anyone setting out in the opposite direction, away from life, has to look forwards, towards death. Maybe, in such cases, a letter can be a glance in the wrong direction, a glance back at life, at your loved ones, that risks rooting you to the spot.

But Daniel hadn't yet lived. He hadn't had a chance to live life to the full. He wasn't mourning anything he'd lost; he hadn't yet found anything that he loved that much—that meant such a lot to him that he couldn't have stood the longing. Or had he?

Did Daniel's longing have an object? Did he know how he wanted to love or live? Did any of us know back then?

Is that what I'm looking for? For the unknown object of Daniel's longing or the origin of his exile? For the beginning of desire? Perhaps I am looking for it because it's still a mystery to me how I managed to discover my own desire at that time and in that milieu. Perhaps because I wonder whether Daniel had discovered what he was longing for, but couldn't have what he desired. Or was it that he didn't know what to look for?

Perhaps, though, I am looking for this exile because I still come across it today, in all the countries I travel to, especially, but not only, in Muslim countries—in all religious and traditional places where all that still exists: the nameless wanting, the speechless search for a longing of one's own, the unmentionable sexuality. Perhaps I am writing about it because it isn't over yet, because those of us who desire slightly differently shouldn't feel so sure of ourselves, because we should think of all those who want to love like us and can't, because Daniel's story continues to repeat itself.

Perhaps because I want to pit a story against the silence of back then—a story that wouldn't only be Daniel's, but also that of everyone who is looking for a story to live today.

—

Little dishes of crisps and peanut puffs had been set out all over the room. I expect that Daniel's mother had got everything ready that afternoon. She worked in the garden nursery with her husband, managing the office work, taking orders, organising deliveries and keeping records of the gardens that needed regular maintenance. She also provided board for the two young employees and made sure that Daniel's father didn't make excessive demands on their son—that he had enough time left for his studies and wasn't swallowed by his garden work. She was beautiful and strong—a small, lively woman with the same green eyes as her son, whom she adored. The house was next to the nursery, out in the country, so Daniel always had to catch a bus and a train to get to school.

On the table there was pasta salad with diced ham and gherkin and lashings of mayonnaise. There was no alcohol yet, only bottles of Coke and Fanta, but Daniel knew the exact shelf in the wooden wall cupboard where the bottle of rum was kept. Daniel had been invited to all the parties in those first years of secondary school. Although he was quiet, he was always there. He was physically slightly more mature than the rest of us and slightly stronger than the other boys. His hands were slim but long and I was struck by his shoulders, which were absolutely straight, as if they'd been drawn with a ruler. But I never stopped to ask myself why his body had developed so early, and Daniel never spoke of his work at the nursery. He never mentioned having to lug sacks of potting compost, or stand in for one or other of the employees for an afternoon. At first he'd helped out with the lighter work: cleaning tools, mucking out the truck, arranging the smaller plants and flowers in beds and pots, making trellises for climbers, pricking out seedlings. Later he'd helped prune roses and rhododendrons, plant shrubs and trees, mow and scarify the lawns in his father's customers' gardens.

The music came from a Dual record player and in those first years it was as indiscriminate as our first physical advances. We hadn't yet realised that there were different genres and scenes. We had no aesthetic or political criteria; we heard Pink Floyd and the Beach Boys, Barclay James Harvest and the Rolling Stones, ABBA and Fleetwood Mac. The only distinction we made was based on the songs' practical use—fast pieces to get us in the mood and slow pieces for close dancing. In our world, the Stones' 'Wild Horses' was interchangeable with 'Michelle'.

It grew darker and there were more slow songs. We changed partners with each new song and danced with everybody, holding each other close. There was no permanent pairing off, there were no hierarchies, no degrees of closeness; we waited for the ballads and then we pressed up against one another and felt each other's bodies, one by one. It was like with the bark of the trees; you had to try to feel the differences. Pressing my body up against a boy's, I'd close my eyes the way I did in the woods and use my sense of touch to discover what set him apart—whether he was slim or brawny, what his breath felt like, how tight he held me, how snugly our bodies fitted together, the way our knees touched when we slow danced—our hips—how warm it got.

And then we'd kiss. That was part of it; we always kissed at these close-dance parties—and we always kissed everyone, without exception. It would never have occurred to us that it was maybe strange to kiss everyone. We had no notion of intimacy as something exclusive—something *intimate*—that two people might want to discover alone, with each other, for each other. It wasn't a conscious decision. It wasn't a political conviction—that eroticism should be communal or love shared out democratically. We had no convictions. Nor was it something we talked about. We invented rules and rituals and thought they were normal, and we copied rules and rituals and thought we'd invented them.

And so I kissed my way through the possibilities, feeling my way blindly through the various lips—wet lips, open lips, greedy lips, hard or soft lips, lips waiting like the hollow in the beech tree. I felt the differences—how some things felt better than others, the different ways of touching a boy with my mouth and body—and I discovered, too, how some boys suddenly changed, or seemed to me to change, stretching and flexing, unfurling and opening up to reveal someone quite different from the person I had known before.

—

The books lay open in front of us and we pored over the schematic diagrams. We raised our eyes, without looking at anyone, just to avoid being caught staring at the books for too long, and then we lowered them again, just to avoid being looked at—to avoid having to catch someone's eye and hold it. None of us was sure how best to conceal this mixture of shame and curiosity, but we all thought the others knew. The exaggerated joviality of our teacher was a troubling indication that he wasn't at ease either. Studied casualness was never a good sign.

It was impossible to say when or why 'sex education' had begun to be called 'sex education' rather than 'enlightenment'.[2] Maybe our teachers assumed we'd already had 'enlightening' talks with our parents, and now the state-school version of the facts of life was to give what we knew a scientific touch. In the seventies, mind you, 'sex ed' was taught so early on that parents hardly had a chance to be the first to 'enlighten' their children. Perhaps the idea was to teach us that 'enlightenment' always lags behind events.

At any rate, we'd all had our first primary-school sex-ed lessons by the time the subject was on the agenda again at secondary school. It was presumably something of an achievement that young people were, if only in theory, regarded as sexual beings at all. It was presumably a historical advance that sexuality should even be discussed. I don't suppose our teachers' generation had ever talked about sexuality, either with their parents or with their teachers. We should probably have been grateful that taboos were being broken like this, at a state school. The only thing was, there was no mention of sexuality in sex-education lessons.

'Sex education' dealt purely with the mechanics of reproduction. Our text books contained schematic diagrams showing cross sections of male and female bodies. Thin arrows indicated the organs and genitalia as if to show a surgeon's assistants where to put the clips for an operation. Everything was neatly labelled and numbered; each part had a name and a mechanical or biological function. Maybe those biological functions explain why sex ed was part of biology. Given the schematic nature of the illustrations, which looked, with all their tubes and pipes, like cross sections of car engines, it might just as well have been taught in physics. The aesthetics were those of a construction kit and the teaching resembled an instruction manual. The difference was that our teachers didn't instruct us in the workings of these particular instruments so that we could use them; they explained how they worked so that we *wouldn't* use them.

It was a pedagogical puzzle. We were supposed to learn how our bodies join together, how the fluids merge, how arousal is discharged, what pattern the rhythm of conception follows, how to count the days when pregnancy is possible—all in order to prevent conception. That was what sex ed was really about: the mechanics of reproduction and the prevention of pregnancy. We were told how we could get pregnant so that we wouldn't. Strangely enough, I can't remember being taught about methods of contraception, about condoms or the pill. The main thing was that we knew what our bodies were capable of if we let them—so that we'd make damn sure we didn't let them.

It was eloquent helplessness. There was no mention of pleasure or lust, of the various ways of loving your way into someone else's body, the desire to lose yourself, the craving for more—no mention of different forms of touch, different kinds of satisfaction, or of the thirst that keeps on growing, the more you drink. We were entering a period of emotional and physical upheaval: our bodies were developing lives of their own; we were at the mercy of emotions we had no words to describe, driven along by desire without knowing where we were going, like animals with no sense of smell, forever turning and changing, clumsy, confused by our lack of bearings. We were discovering our bodies, but mainly we were discovering that they no longer felt like ours: they looked different, they were metamorphosing, adopting new rhythms, suddenly present, visible, palpable. This was us and yet we sensed that we no longer knew ourselves.

And all anyone taught us at that time was the structural organisation of the human body, and the mechanics of erection and penetration that lead to pregnancy.

Nobody provided us with words to help us form some kind of picture, explore sexual pleasure or develop an erotic language. Nobody explained that desire is a river without banks. Nobody told us that swimming in that river feels like letting yourself drift, or that sex, unlike the neat diagrams in our textbooks, is a messy business where everything gets wet, where you get covered in sweat and blood, drenched in juices from all the orifices and pores of the body, until you seem to dissolve in them. Nobody told us that there were notions and ideas about desire and sexuality that had nothing to do with either. Nobody explained our fantasies. Nobody freed us from the pressure, the compulsion to be faster, more precocious, cooler, bigger, more advanced than the others.

Nobody mentioned masturbation or the various ways of discovering yourself and what you want. Nobody spoke of sexual practices whose aim is pleasure rather than conception. I can't remember orgasms (the mere implications of the plural!) being mentioned. 'Ejaculation', of course, and 'ovulation'. But 'orgasm'?

It was presumably regarded as particularly liberal to talk about sexuality in school without mentioning love, spiritual kinship, storks or angels. It was presumably supposed to be courageous and anticlerical to teach sexuality separately from religious doctrine and marriage. I loved my school. To this day I am grateful for what was sown and cultivated in me during my years there. My philosophy teacher, my German teacher, my history teacher and later tutor—they were all, without exception, marvellously committed teachers who did their best to give us a moral and political grounding. But talk of sexuality was at once progressive and backwards. Ultimately, the religious discourse was simply replaced by a biologistic one, and the way in which sexuality was constantly coupled with pregnancy in order to prevent pregnancy spawned more fear than any Catholic teaching would ever have been capable of. It wasn't the sinful nature of lust that was to make us fear sexuality, but its dangerous consequences. Sexuality was no longer a vice; it was a threat.

—

When do we become adults? Does adulthood have a clear-cut beginning, at a fixed point in time? When did our experiences stop belonging to childhood? How was it determined? And who decided?

People talk of 'coming of age' and it's a mystery to me what they mean—becoming an adult, emerging from puberty, discovering your sexuality—or all those things at once? What age do you come of? And how do you come of it?

Religions have invented rites and traditions to define coming of age as a threshold, an important transition, past which a young person is believed—or expected—to have reached religious maturity. At bar or bat mitzvah and at confirmation, for instance, families and communities hold initiation celebrations for their young people, declaring them adults in a one-off act. Reading the *maftir* portion from the Torah or saying the Christian creed is not only a way of passing religious tradition down through the generations; it is also a speech act that transforms the child into an adult.

That all this, to put it profanely, is a colossal misunderstanding, is brought home to us by the young people's frequent inability to appreciate their relatives' gifts— valuable and beautiful presents such as silver spoons or reference works—things that any educated middle-class adult would be delighted with, but that mean little to children whose notion of happiness is more fleeting than the gifts allow for.

So when is religious maturity said to begin? What are the requirements? At what point are young people considered mature?

In Judaism, coming of age is defined as the ability to obey the commandments. Similarly, the Talmud regards children as adults when they understand consequences: only when you grasp the meaning of the words you speak can you know whether you are obeying Jewish rules and commandments or breaking them. In principle, the Talmud regards girls as capable of understanding the commandments from the age of eleven, and boys from the age of twelve, though it's considered more certain once the girls are twelve and the boys thirteen. But for some rabbis, the age limit alone is not enough; they prefer to rely on physical signs to identify coming of age. The intellectual ability to understand one's own words and vows is no longer the only relevant factor for them; 'signs of puberty' suddenly play a decisive role. A boy is said to be a minor as long as he 'has not yet grown two hairs'.

Why should religious maturity be bound up with sexual maturity? Because in sexual matters, too, it might be a good idea to be able to judge the consequences of our words and actions?

'Half-ripe fig'—that's the expression used for an adolescent girl in the Babylonian Talmud: 'The sages use metaphor to describe the ages of woman: an unripe fig, a half-ripe fig and a ripe fig.' An unripe fig is a child, a half-ripe fig is a young girl and a ripe fig is a 'manable' woman whose 'father no longer has any power over her'.[3]

I suspect I'd have liked it if I'd been called 'half ripe' when I was an adolescent. 'Manable' was not something I aspired to be, but I'd have liked the ambivalence of semi-ripeness, and whether half ripe or ripe, I would have been adamant that my father should have no power over me, ever.

Muslims, similarly, stipulate the moment when young people may be regarded as *baligh*, when they are mature enough for the laws of faith—often the onset of menstruation in girls and the appearance of pubic hair in boys. As far as I know, no ritual celebration of any form has emerged to make this moment more visible in Islam, but all religions posit this threshold, this moment when sexual and religious maturity supposedly coincide, and which is arbitrarily declared the transition to adulthood.

A similar notion in our secondary school meant that

we were told that our teachers would no longer address us by our first names once we'd been confirmed—as if their respect for us pupils were somehow tied up with our profession of Christian faith. In fact, nobody stuck to this announcement—perhaps because we were confirmed when we were only thirteen and our intellectual and religious immaturity was only too apparent, or perhaps because our young atheist teachers rejected the tradition anyway.

Religious and nonreligious societies agree in regarding the transition into adulthood not as a process or development, but as a clearly delineated moment. In Latin America, female maturity is often celebrated at the *fiesta de quince*, on a girl's fifteenth birthday. In Bali, ritual coming-of-age celebrations are held when a girl gets her first period or when a boy's voice breaks. In Korea, there is an official coming-of-age day in the third week of May.

But what if coming of age and puberty don't coincide? What if they are out of sync with each other? And what if, instead of discovering our sexuality only once, during puberty, we discover it again later—and then again, after that? What if our sexuality reinvents itself every time our desire shifts, every time the object of our desire changes? What if the nature of our desire is constantly changing—growing deeper, lighter, wilder, more reckless, more tender, more selfish, more devoted, more radical?

I'm not sure that religious maturity has anything

to do with sexual maturity, but I suspect that faith, like desire, can be discovered more than once—that in faith, as in desire, subjectivity is continuously changing shape—that it is something dynamic, searching, ever-shifting, ever-deepening. And I suspect that with faith, too, it is less important what you believe than how you believe, because it is the capacity to give yourself—to abandon yourself—to someone or something that testifies to depth.

The expression 'coming of age', on the other hand, presupposes an act, a one-off event, a single form of desire that need be identified only once. Traditional coming-of-age rites reduce desire to something like sexual initiation, and go no further. Seen in this way, sexuality doesn't change; it is constant, shaping lives and forming what appear to be clearly defined beings. Convenient categories such as 'heterosexuality', 'homosexuality', 'bisexuality' and 'transsexuality' suggest moreover that forms of love and practices of desire solidify into stable, lifelong identities. Stories about discovering desire tend to be set in adolescence and invariably have linear plots from which a single form of desire emerges—a desire focused not on any kind of pleasure, but on an identity that suppos-edly reaffirms itself with every sexual encounter.

But is it really like that?

I went through adolescence at the same time as Daniel, but Daniel never made the transition to adult-hood; he was dead by then, and whatever marks that threshold, he never crossed it. As for me, I didn't discover my desire just the once; rather I developed desire—or desire developed me—many times over, and each time slightly differently. New forms of lust and desire formed around the earlier ones, like rings on a tree trunk, years after I had left school, years after Daniel had taken his life.

We didn't live in sync, Daniel and I; we didn't reach erotic maturity at the same time; the stories of our desire can't be told in parallel. But my search for the sources of the self is tied up with Daniel; my questions about Daniel led me to search for the prerequisites for (a different) desire. How were we to understand what we felt when we didn't know that it existed? How were we supposed to voice our desire when there were no words for that desire, no pictures, no models? How anything distinct emerges from those murky years—anything that speaks to us, that we want to live as adults—generally remains something of a mystery.

'Coming of age' presupposes individual development, as if adolescence took place in a void, as if it were purely up to us how fast or slow, happy or unhappy our sexual awakening. It suggests a story without a context, as if we could grow up into whatever we wanted—as if want didn't come along in prefabricated forms, as if the social, political and aesthetic limits of the world in which we live didn't all too often determine the limits of our imagination.

—

It was music that showed me the way to my desire. Not literature, not film—music. To be more precise, the complexity of musical experience back then at school laid trails for the sexual pleasure that I wouldn't discover until many years later. At a time when nobody spoke of different kinds of desire, of homosexuality or bisexuality, the language of music revealed to me all that I would later experience erotically. I don't suppose that was quite what our music teacher Herr Kossarinsky had in mind, but I am grateful to him to this day, and more than that, I realise, looking back, that music opened up horizons to me that made it possible for me to survive—horizons that Daniel can't ever have found.

Music lessons were held in a special room—a small, modern hall with coloured glass in the windows, green velvet curtains and a low, single-level stage with a green blackboard on wheels and a Bösendorfer grand piano. La la la la, up the scale, la, la, laa, down the scale. Our music teacher sat at the piano, and we sang the scales that he played. La la la la, up the scale, and la, la, laa, down again—each time a tone higher: la la la la, up the scale, la la laa, down. Another tone higher. Herr Kossarinsky was a cheerful man, though serious. He was always correctly dressed and could be strict, but he took a playful, sensuous pleasure in his work. He was never without a small brown leather briefcase where he kept his scores and cassettes; this he would balance on the handlebars of his bike when he rode to school. On some afternoons, after choir or orchestra practice, when he was particularly satisfied with the sound we had produced, he would perform tricks. He'd swing himself onto his bicycle backwards, sit with his bottom on the handlebars, his hands on the grips and his feet back-to-front on the pedals, and pedal away with great spirit and good humour, his head turned to look over his shoulder. All attempts to imitate him failed painfully.

Kossarinsky took it in turns with another music teacher to run the school choir. He was also responsible for the orchestra, the big band and—fortunately for me— our year's music lessons. He arranged pieces in his spare time, transposed music for every ensemble in the school, organised instruments for children who were musically gifted but financially hard up, accompanied us on the piano at school concerts and sometimes played the organ at the local Protestant church on Sundays and holidays, instead of the choirmaster.

'All right, and now again, with a little more oomph!' Kossarinsky looked at the boys in the front row who thought themselves too cool for morning singing. He had no intention of handing out the music early to avoid their bored looks. La la la la, up the scale, la la laa, down. He played energetically, as if it were the most exciting thing in the world, listening as we got ourselves into voice, and probing the individual voices for clarity, like a wine connoisseur hunting about in a dusty, overfilled cellar for a lucky find. After a while, the first of us began to drop out, unable to reach the notes; that way Kossarinsky gradually sussed out our vocal ranges even before we were properly aware that such a thing existed.

Coming into the music room, we had sat down wherever we felt like sitting, higgledy-piggledy, following our likes and dislikes—a motley bunch. Now Kossarinsky handed out the music, pressing it into the hand of each of us with a smile, sometimes shocking the unrulier pupils into silence with a cheeky comment. Then he returned to the piano, played the tune and got us to sing it after him, reading the music or singing by ear.

Each lesson began in the same way: getting ourselves into voice, warming up, singing scales and intervals. Then we'd sing a song—folk songs at first, and then Bach, Mendelssohn, Schumann, Schubert. To begin with, we all sang in unison; later Kossarinsky split up the class. The world divided again. Again girls and boys were separated, but this time it was by voice, not sex; this time there was a reason. And we weren't just split in two, or only at first; later, when the boys' voices had broken, we fanned out into four groups. This wasn't about who anyone thought we were or ought to be; it was about the way we sounded, whether we were soprano, alto, tenor or bass. It didn't matter what sex we were; what mattered was our voice, our range. Kossarinsky didn't divide us up; he divided us *into* groups, to create a new, many-voiced sound.

—

These days I often travel to countries where the circles of my childhood are still being drawn. I visit places where the divisions and separations based on sex and sexuality are reiterated and reinforced—those unspoken codes and conventions that mark out the terrain where people are to speak and live and love. The circles are different and the boundaries are different; they are coloured by culture and overwritten by religion—but such nuances make no difference to the structures of exclusion and containment, or to the way in which the spaces inside the circles change to fit the outer lines; they make no difference to the unmentionable nature of the spaces in between or to the invisibility of those who inhabit them.

On one of my last trips to Gaza I had planned to visit a district of Gaza City inhabited mainly by supporters of Islamic jihad. It happened to be the day when two Palestinian women were released from Israeli captivity. They'd already had the official Hamas reception and were due to arrive home at any minute. Where I was, outside the house of one of these women, everything was ready: the men were gathered on the street, the older ones sitting on white plastic chairs, the younger ones standing on the pavement; huge black loudspeakers were blasting out triumphal music, photos of the homecomer had pride of place in the entranceway, and the staircase was hung with brightly coloured balloons. In public, martial symbolism had centre stage, but inside, in private, everything was infused with pink, childlike joy. For the men, a heroine of the resistance was returning home; for the women, the homecomer was first and foremost a daughter, a niece, a sister.

My interpreter, Hala, was a young, unveiled Palestinian woman with shoulder-length black hair. That's a rare sight in Gaza these days. In the years since Hamas came to power, unveiled women have almost completely vanished from the streets. Few women venture into public uncovered, and robes, dresses and coats are getting longer too; a mere headscarf isn't enough any more; the *niqab*, the black facial veil, worn in combination with a *chador*, a long cloak, has become the norm, especially in an area like this, largely populated by Islamic jihad supporters.

I usually have a scarf with me, something I can use to improvise a head covering if courtesy demands. It never quite works out; there's always an unruly tuft of hair sticking out somewhere. Covering my head is a friendly gesture of accommodation, a citation of a norm that invariably goes awry. Sometimes I wear a close-fitting hat under the veil to stop my hair from escaping and to save myself endless faffing around, but this little hat of mine bears a suspicious resemblance to the headgear often worn by men in Muslim countries, which makes the combination of hat and headscarf even more bizarre.

'Don't we need veils?' I asked Hala, worried that it might be particularly impolite to appear in this devout neighbourhood with bare heads—especially on a day of celebration. It was no problem, Hala assured me, she was with me, wasn't she? That wasn't what I'd asked; I was as much concerned about myself as about her. But her only thought was that my presence excused her own uncon- ventionality. It was, in any case, too late; we were already in the middle of the passageway outside the front door, thronged by all the people going in and out, their eyes turned on us in astonishment because we were the only ones there who were neither bearded nor veiled.

We were told we could go in. The women in the courtyard looked like a dark mass, indistinguishable in their black robes, shapeless, bodiless, a surging, impen- etrable wall of cloth, without hair or faces or more than tiny patches of skin—people who were nothing but eyes and hands, and all moving constantly. As is the custom, Hala asked around until she found Ahlam, the lady of the house, to find out whether I might speak to her. Hala introduced us, but as I held out my hand to take Ahlam's under her *chador*, she suddenly started back and my hand missed hers, slipped and touched her black clad elbow. It was an awkward moment. Failed greetings are nearly as embarrassing as clumsy goodbyes. But it was such a crush; there was always someone jostling somewhere; in all the mayhem, it was no wonder our hands had missed each other. We went upstairs, passing countless women carrying plastic carafes of cordial, or trays of small glasses of sweet tea to the guests standing on the stairs or out on the street.

Upstairs, Ahlam eventually stopped beside a group of women. Soon they were standing around me in a semi-circle and we were able to talk. What had previously looked like a homogeneous black mass now fanned out to reveal distinct shapes, individuals, pairs of eyes. They talked animatedly, interrupting one another to tell me about their lives in Gaza; they gave me their opinions on Hamas and Islamic jihad, and on Gilad Shalit, the Israeli soldier who was still being held in Gaza, and had become a miserable bargaining chip between Hamas and the Israeli government. They felt sorry for the young Israeli's mother and knew what she was going through; they'd worried, too, when their children were in Israeli captivity—and as we stood there talking, by the oblique route of Hala's translation and always with a slight time lag, they suddenly began to giggle. Hala was no longer translating, but talking to them directly, apparently about me.

'They want to know if you're a girl or a boy...' Hala explained, slightly sheepishly. All eyes stared at me, riveted, waiting to see how I'd react. They were nervous, afraid they might have offended me with their question—but more than anything, they were curious to hear my answer.

I like questions like that. They are rarely asked in this part of the world. Frank questions are swallowed here, covered up, suppressed by a normalised acceptance that is so terrified of stepping on anyone's toes that it ends up keeping everyone at arm's length. The enlightened heterosexual majority claims tolerance, though there's nothing to tolerate; people boast about their friendships with homosexuals but never talk about what friends really speak about, namely sex. A lot of people act understanding, but don't understand much because they don't dare ask questions. Being curious, finding out about other people, exploring common ground and differences—all that disappears under the heavy cloak of well-meaning tolerance that prefers to leave everything vague and would rather tolerate the unknown than run the risk of getting to know it and finding it frighteningly attractive or repellent, understandable or incomprehensible, surprising or boring. As long as that goes on, homosexuals will remain a monolithic block, rather than fanning out, like the women behind their veils, to reveal individual stories and experiences.

'They want to know if you're a girl or a boy...'

The other reason I like such questions is that they seem to me serious. I certainly don't find them offensive;

47

the sensitivity with which some people react to questions about our sexuality is alien to me. It's as if every question about sexual orientation were an insult in itself, and more than that, it's as if questions about our desire were easy to answer, as if it were unequivocal, settled, incontrovertible, as if desire weren't constantly changing and expanding, as if it were something you could control, trim to size, force in one direction or another, as if it weren't justified to ask why we love one way or another, what difference it makes, how long we've known, whether we're sure…

'Ask them what they think I look like.' I watched Hala translating my words into Arabic, then they all talked at once and Hala had to wait for them to agree among themselves before translating their reply: 'You're wearing trousers and you have short hair and that looks like a boy, but when you laugh and talk, it's clear that you're a girl.'

I had to laugh—partly to show them I didn't mind their doubts, but also because it was a lovely description and one in which I recognised myself. It was only now that I realised what had happened when I'd been introduced to Ahlam. She hadn't withdrawn her hand by mistake; she had taken me for a boy—what else was she to think when she saw someone with short hair? It wasn't that she disapproved of women with short hair; she simply had no idea that women *could* have short hair. That it was an aesthetic option for a woman to look like me was unthinkable to her—it was beyond the bounds of possibility, beyond the bounds of what she considered possible. I must be a man. When I'd held out my hand, she had been afraid that I, a man, would touch her illicitly.

The story of the women in Gaza makes clear that it's not just words, but also norms and conventions, symbols and gestures that depend on the use that is made of them. It is all too easy to suppose that Ahlam's refusal to shake hands with me and the women's boy-or-girl question was in some way linked up with moral or ideological disapproval. But the women didn't reject me as a woman; they simply didn't *recognise* me as a woman. That's not a matter of ideology; it's a matter of understanding. They didn't know any women with short hair and trousers. I embodied none of the symbolic or aesthetic codes of femininity; they couldn't see the woman in me.

In the eighties, when the Mafia was in control of every aspect of Sicilian life and culture, long before fearless lawyers and police officers had begun to take action against the cartels, a member of the Mafia presented himself to the local police in Palermo and said he'd come to make a statement. He wanted to give himself up, tell them about all the crimes he knew of and cooperate with the authorities. The police officers committed this honest Mafioso to a psychiatric asylum—anyone who claimed he wanted to make a statement against the Mafia must be crazy. It wasn't an act of repression; they genuinely believed he was mad.

That's how ideologies work, but the worlds in which we live work like that too, not just in Gaza, but also in Paderborn or Palermo. They establish rules and ideas; they create practices and convictions that seem natural to everyone—given rather than constructed—and they mark out boundaries that mustn't be crossed: boundaries of reason and shame, boundaries of dress and hairstyles—boundaries that seem self-evident and indispensable to everyone.

I wondered whether to explain to Ahlam that I'd never have tried to give her my hand if I'd been a man—that of course I wouldn't have wanted to violate the traditional boundaries of shame. Perhaps she was wondering in the same instant whether to explain to me that of course she'd have given me her hand if she'd known I was a woman—that she'd never have shunned contact with me.

Neither of us said anything.

—

When I was at school, religion was a cut-and-dried affair. There were no Muslims in our class; we were more or less evenly divided into Protestants and Catholics—and then there was one Jewish boy. For the compulsory RE lessons during the first years of secondary school, before pupils were given the choice between RE and philosophy, the Protestants among us were taught by an all-out atheist theologian who regarded RE as lit crit, and the Catholics were sent to the local priest who regarded RE as catechism. The Jewish boy, meanwhile, had a free period and was allowed to go to the Italian ice-cream shop. Because we were split into two groups, though, it was a long time before anyone realised he was Jewish; the Protestants thought he was Catholic and the Catholics thought he must be Protestant. As a result, nobody missed him and he didn't stand out as different.

Religion drew no boundaries. It mattered more whether you chose to do modern languages or classics. In our third year at secondary school the class was divided, ostensibly according to academic interest, but in fact, more often than not, according to our parents' social class and educational background, each successful generation spawning the next. I didn't pay particular attention at the time, but I'd be very surprised if any of the pupils who chose to do classics hadn't come from a well-educated middle-class family.

Cutter sailing and tennis marked another social divide. The boys who went cutter sailing on the river at the weekend would often sit and talk on the shore together afterwards; sometimes they'd finish off with a football match on the sand. They dreamt of becoming shipbuilders or sailing around the world and they smelt more reckless and exciting than the others whose spirit of adventure went no further than getting a bit of red dust on their white tennis shoes.

I wanted to go camping with Jakob, one of the boys who went cutter sailing, and Markus, another boy from school. We had an orange tent that we put up at the bottom of the garden, on the edge of the woods. My mother thought it perfectly normal that I wanted to spend the night in a tent with two boys from my school and we thought it perfectly normal, too, until the three of us were rolling around on the floor of the tent that night and I was hugging and kissing sometimes one, sometimes the other and sometimes both at once—and letting them kiss me. Eventually I decided on Jakob and we touched each other, almost limp with desire, and helpless too, because we didn't have any idea what we wanted, or how we were meant to know how to want, or how to touch each other to give each other pleasure—or indeed if that was really what we wanted, to *give pleasure*. It just came over us. Perhaps it was more curiosity than desire, more excitement than lust. It excited us to feel each other's nakedness, to run our hands over each other's skin, not just the places that were normally covered by clothes, but all over, running our hands up and down each other's bodies, exploring everything, all the hollows and hiding places, all the parts that had no names, that were unpronounceable, but existed, there in the dark, and could be touched. I moved as if treading on the floes of the frozen river, afraid that the ice might give way beneath me. I tried to make myself light, with every touch of my fingers, every movement that brought me closer to the forbidden place, listening intently for any sign of cracks that might open up and pull me down. In the end, I got right into Jakob's sleeping bag and stayed there.

The next morning we were shaken and speechless—just as speechless as during the night, only that at night we hadn't thought much of it, whereas now the fear of discovery spread like sand, trickling into the spaces between us, filling in the cracks, clogging up apertures, obscuring our sight and making it hard to swallow. It wasn't clear what exactly had happened, but that morning it felt as if things had gone too far, things that hadn't been planned. In a way, it was true; we had evidently touched each other as far as we dared—but we'd have dared more if we'd known how.

The limits of our pleasure were still defined by the limits of our imagination. We had no idea what was supposed to happen afterwards; our hands and lips were inexperienced—but that wasn't the worst; we also had no idea—we couldn't imagine—what we might want. But maybe that isn't true. Maybe back then, the limits of our pleasure were also still defined by the limits of our desire. Maybe we just weren't driven enough by desire yet, maybe we were still exploring more than anything else, maybe it was curiosity that drove us rather than desire. Maybe.

—

We lay flat in the bushes in the woods, waiting for passers-by, a bulging bag of dried peas on the leaves beside us, heaped around with earth to keep it from tipping over at the crucial moment when we would search frantically for ammunition. We had started off lying on the bridge shooting at cars, but it was too risky on the road.

Markus had once got a slap in the face for playing pranks on drivers. On that occasion we'd been dropping water bombs on car rooftops. We stood on the bridge watching the cars round the bend; the road began to climb after that, so that even before they came into view we could tell locals from strangers by the sound of their engines. Strangers to the area didn't know to shift down a gear before the bend, and so the noise of a furiously revving engine would alert us to our next victim.

We were standing on the side of the bridge facing the hill with our backs to the drivers, waiting for them to drive into the dark maw below us. Then, when they re-emerged from under the bridge on the other side, we'd drop our plump balloons on the car roofs. You couldn't really miss and it made an almighty smack. We'd been at it all day, running to the house to fill new balloons with water and then running back through the woods to our ambush. I'd just landed a particularly fine hit and we were still gloating as we looked down the hill again to spot the next car, when suddenly there was the driver, standing in front of us on the bridge, fuming. We hadn't noticed him stop his car at the top of the hill and take the road down through the woods. I dashed off the bridge, slipped into the bushes and made straight for the den, not turning round or stopping until I'd crawled all the way in and was lying under the fallen fir tree. Then I looked back at the bridge.

Markus was standing there all alone, bewildered and frightened. I ran back to him, but it was too late; the driver had clouted him one and gone back to his car without hanging around. I felt wretched. Not because I'd thrown the water bomb or given the driver a shock, but because Markus had got a slap in the face that by rights was mine.

This time, then, we were lying in the bushes in the middle of the woods with our peashooters, but the only passers-by were elderly couples, and we didn't want to shoot at them. Suddenly there was a rustling behind us and, twisting our heads without getting up, we saw a huge boxer dog, frenziedly turning this way and that, sniffing here and there, and going round in circles, apparently unable to decide which way to go. It was a powerful animal, athletically built, its ribcage bulging, the muscles and sinews of its hind legs clearly visible, and it went round and round, as if it were looking for something. We couldn't work out what it was doing there; most dogs stayed on the path with their owners. The bushes off the path were our realm, especially here in our hiding place, where we were lying in wait. The boxer ran on a little way, sniffing out the territory as if trying to catch something. It was panting, exuding unbridled energy like a heady scent, and when it shook its muzzle, half sneezing, half spitting the drool from its chops and still moving frenetically, it was suddenly frightening. Something about the dog repelled us, scared us, although there was nothing unusual or strange about it; it definitely wasn't dangerous and didn't look like a fighting dog. There was nothing suspicious, nothing threatening, but still it gave us the creeps.

Intuitively, without stopping to talk about it, we took up our peashooters, quietly grabbed a handful of peas from the bag and each popped a pea in our mouths. We moistened the peas, pushed them into the opening of the pipes with our tongues, levelled the peashooters at the dog, shot—and missed. The boxer had turned away from us, its muzzle deep in scents we couldn't smell. It was perhaps six or seven metres off; we saw it from behind, saw its testicles between its wiry legs, took aim—and missed again. We made a plan. One of us would aim at the dog's anus, exposed beneath its docked tail—and the other at its testicles. I clearly remember the mixture of fear and aggression I felt and I remember the sight of that closely shorn dog and its body that suddenly stood for something I couldn't have named, that triggered something I wanted rid of. Markus and I were potentiating our fear of our own impotence as we shot our dried peas at the boxer's testicles. We didn't know whether the dog would identify us as its aggressors. We shot at our repulsion, our arousal, our fear, until we hit and the boxer started up—once, twice—like an animal that's touched an electric fence. Then, not knowing where the pain had come from, it bounded off.

We lay, quietly trembling, on the ground. A short time elapsed, then we picked up our peashooters in silence. We left the bag of peas where it was; we didn't want them any more. And without looking at each other, without exchanging a word, we trotted home.

I never used a peashooter again. It was over.

—

The invisible had always existed. Pain was invisible—at least to begin with, creeping up from within you, insinuating itself into your limbs and gradually distorting them. Illness was invisible, stealing painlessly into your blood and destroying it a little at a time. But the healer's medicine was invisible too. The healer lived in a high-rise estate on the outskirts of town; she treated a wart on my wrist, and the dead relatives she invoked as she circled her hand around my arm were also invisible—as was, a few weeks later, the wart itself, which disappeared from one day to the next, leaving not so much as a bump or a discoloration on my skin, as if there had never been anything there. Invisible, too, were the gifts of the *curandera*, the Native American healer in Argentina who nursed us children when we had poisoned ourselves, and whom our mother trusted implicitly, with a trust that was communicated to us without the need for comprehension.

Metaphysics was invisible, and yet seemed so self-evident that the question of how you could believe in something invisible didn't even arise. This metaphysical mode of thought implies, as Jean Améry once pointed out, a certain independence from the visible order of things, an unquestioned sense of security beyond all actual experience in the real world, a kind of invulnerability. Like love and musicality, such belief is intangible, not something you can make up your mind to or give reasons for. If you attempt to explain why you love someone by pointing out your loved one's qualities, or listing similarities and points in common, you are only producing reasons after the fact—mere illustrations or symptoms of love—because there can ultimately be no reasons for love; it happens, it takes hold of us, it is its own justification, its own silent evidence. Metaphysical belief is the same. Like love or musicality, such intimacy with invisible things is a blessing you can neither demand nor reject.

The first time I travelled to Jerusalem, it astonished me that all the narrative elements of the Bible—the Garden of Gethsemane and its olive trees, the Via Dolorosa—that all that *existed*. The materiality which others saw as confirmation of their faith was repellent to me; it detracted from the imaginary power of the narrative. I felt robbed of something; the story and my imagining of it seemed diminished. The invisible was an unquestioned reality free from the need for visible evidence and closely bound up with the certainty that something can exist and influence your life without having to assume physical form.

When we were children, all the feast days revolved around the invisible. St Nicholas brought his gifts at night and vanished, leaving only traces of his presence—almonds and mandarins. The Christ Child came but remained behind closed doors and could only be heard if he accidentally knocked one of his wings against the bell on the Christmas tree. And the Easter bunny certainly couldn't be seen, even if my brother tried in vain to get through to me with none-too-subtle hints that it was sitting at the breakfast table with me. Invisibility was the existential attribute of these beings—they couldn't be sitting anywhere with me. The Disneyfied version of Easter popular today, where huge plush bunnies lollop around public parks, anthropomorphised into bipeds because the actors inside the furry costumes can't be expected to go on all fours, was unthinkable in those days. The same goes for the currently ubiquitous paedophile version of a bearded Father Christmas with a big jute sack, an old man sweating inside his felt coat while children sit on his lap and are asked what they want for Christmas—unthinkable.

But there was also another kind of invisibility. It wasn't part of the nature of things; it was constructed.

There was no mention of homosexuality in my childhood. It existed—there were people who were homosexual, but for us children they didn't figure, either in real life or in fiction. They never became visible—not as homosexuals anyway.

They were like shapes in a join-the-dots picture, made up of individual characteristics, of detached codes that had to be pieced together in the beholder's mind. You couldn't see the complete outline. The individual allusions didn't make up a picture; it was only when the signs were joined up in the imagination that 'a homosexual' came into being. The word itself was never mentioned. That was the art. Just as all those numbered dots in the join-the-dots books were meant to distract you from what you would find when you connected them—just as the picture remained hidden except as a figment of somebody's imagination—homosexuals didn't ever explicitly exist.

We watched *Laurel and Hardy*, laughing at them because they were a funny couple, but without seeing the parody. We saw only the aesthetic shifts that resulted from the slightly ridiculous nature of these male characters who were effeminate without really being feminine—always faintly absurd in their attempts to perform masculinity, always slightly comical in their failure. We hadn't seen the great Hollywood films of that time. In William Wyler's

1961 movie *The Children's Hour*, with Shirley MacLaine and Audrey Hepburn, homosexuality doesn't feature as homosexuality either; it is present only in the affliction it causes. Desire is still unspoken; it exists, but is visible only as anguish, as an impossibility that makes the characters the victims at once of others' projections and of their own lust. Their particular form of desire, the feature that marks them out as different, is never mentioned.

In my childhood, at my school, in our little world in the seventies and eighties, homosexuals remained obscure. They existed; something was different, but the difference was hidden, unmentionable, so that homosexuals were imagined rather than seen, creatures as invisible as desert field mice, a rare species of fauna—something you might come across in a natural history book but would never glimpse in nature. Martin Dannecker and Reimut Reiche's wonderfully entitled 1974 study 'The Ordinary Homosexual'[4] contested something that didn't exist in our childhood. It wasn't that there weren't any ordinary homosexuals, but that they weren't perceived as such.

Parallel to our childhood, outside our little world, in Berlin and New York, San Francisco and London, other people were waging the battles from which I would later profit, getting beaten up and arrested by the police, protesting against raids and against being tailed. Activists had been fighting for the rights of gays and lesbians for some time, and not just among international artists;

in Germany, too, there was a lively and well-established homosexual scene making a stand against discrimination. The actor Alexander Ziegler was in jail writing *The Consequence*, Rosa von Praunheim was making his films, Hubert Fichte was writing his books—but we knew nothing of any of that. It didn't reach us. For us, homosexuality remained something unreal, nebulous, covert.

The silence surrounding homosexuality was at best disguised as sympathy. You didn't talk about these people; you felt sorry for them, as if they were suffering from a fatal disease. The silence seemed to suggest that they needed protecting—their burden was heavy enough as it was, so everyone let well alone. At worst, they were regarded as curable.

There were of course homosexuals, here and there, but all those who actually existed in our world and lived in our midst—the volleyball teacher, the pharmacist, a neighbour—were stripped of every sign of homosexuality, purged of every unequivocal pointer. An enormous mental effort was made to imagine away homosexuality: a lover everyone knew to be a lover became a 'lodger'; a girlfriend became 'a friend', and 'spare rooms' were fitted out where nobody ever slept, just to keep alive the relatives' belief in chaste sleeping arrangements. Similarly, all burlesque behaviour, however extreme—the over-the-top gestures, the camp posturing, the clothes—all that was simply glossed over.

People went to immense intellectual lengths to put a new spin on the signs—to pass over any visible pointers to real-life homosexuals. What American writer Ralph Ellison wrote about black people in *Invisible Man*—men and women 'of flesh and bone' who went unseen—was true of homosexuals: they remained invisible.

In the fictionalised world of certain cinema and television films of the time, such pointers were aestheticised to produce a 'readable' homosexual, but in our real-life world, in a kind of negative version of the fictional, homosexuals were denied these characteristic features. There were homosexual practices and people who felt homosexual desire, but in the picture conveyed to us when we were children, homosexuals were deprived of precisely those practices and that desire. They were recognised without receiving recognition. Desire and identity were separated. Homosexuals existed, but their homosexuality wasn't acknowledged.

—

There were layers of reality, some easily accessible and others hidden, and anyone interested in the hidden layers had to be taught how to avoid getting sidetracked by the easily accessible—had to be directed not towards phenomena in the world, but towards languages with which to explore those phenomena, to ways of chipping away at the layers and peeling them back to get at other perspectives on reality.

For his first attempt at seducing us into listening, Kossarinsky took Johann Sebastian Bach's Brandenburg Concerto No. 2 in F major. He wrote the work's catalogue number in white chalk on the green music-room blackboard—BWV 1047—and told us the story of its composition.

Then he played the first movement, without explaining anything, without setting us any particular exercise, trusting to the music to take hold of us, to carry us away, leaving us so hungry for more that we would lap up everything he told us in the short break before he played the music a second time. He got us to tell him what we'd heard, and made a list on the blackboard; then he got us to listen again so that we could add to the list. We spotted the solo instruments—trumpet, recorder, violin and oboe—and of course the strings and the *basso continuo*. We didn't just listen; we separated out the various layers of sound in a kind of 'close listening'. The music acquired a depth of focus; it seemed to fan out and develop spatial complexity. Later Kossarinsky got us to do the same close-listening exercise with piano pieces, sometimes pieces we weren't familiar with. He taught us to listen to the left hand—not just the right hand or the melody. This childhood exercise still comes naturally to me; I still listen out for the left hand—and oddly enough not only in music, but in language too. I try to hear the equivalent of the *basso continuo* or left hand in the words of the person I'm talking to—to hear what lies beneath the melody of the spoken word, what sets the rhythm, what accompanies the voice.

Next Kossarinsky introduced us to *ritornello* motifs. He played them on the grand piano: the *tutti* theme in the first eight bars of the first movement, the catchy repetitions of the motifs and then the solo and *tutti* themes in the bars that followed. He played us the solo instruments with their second theme, then he let us hear them in the orchestra. To begin with, he left out harmony and modulations—all that would come later. We were to see what we could hear first, and only then, score in hand, were we to explore the musical architecture. It was like a riddle, like playfully deciphering a language we were learning— even if that wasn't quite what was on the syllabus.

By introducing us to the Brandenburg Concertos, Kossarinsky laid trails for us to follow on our own. He taught us to listen as if listening were a kind of treasure hunt and Bach had hidden clues in the musical terrain. We'd run off in excitement, looking behind each bar as if behind trees, searching for the motifs that Kossarinsky had noted on the blackboard, and crying out in delight when we were the first to solve the clue and spot a motif in its modified form. Meanwhile he taught us about the different kinds of movement and about the quaver motion of Baroque thoroughbass. He played us the sigh motif in the second movement and then got us to listen out for it ourselves.

Finally he fetched another recording of the concerto and we heard the shifts that took place in the music when the same movement was played on old instruments so that the trumpet suddenly seemed less dominant (or less shrill), withdrawing discreetly into the overall sound. Kossarinsky trained us continually to practise listening to music as well as reading it—informed and uninformed listening, different recordings of the same music—and the principle of interpretation became second nature to us. It was through music rather than literature that I learnt what interpretation is and discovered the different ways of reading or approaching a text. The diversity of musical interpretations was to us what the interpretive power of the various exegeses and commentaries of individual passages is to Talmud scholars—the layers of readings that have formed around the original text or Mishnah. Some of the interpretations were yielded by the works of music themselves; others by the different ways of performing them which had, over time, formed around the original compositions. The knowledge that any canonical text, any system of signs can be applied and interpreted differently depending on historical variables and contexts was not a theoretical tenet; it was something we experienced first hand in the world of music.

Over the years, Kossarinsky continued to teach us

close listening, introducing us to the musical languages of various orchestras and of pianists such as Friedrich Gulda, Maurizio Pollini, Vladimir Ashkenazy, Sviatoslav Richter and Vladimir Horowitz.

At the end of that first lesson, Kossarinsky played the Brandenburg Concerto again.

—

How little I know about Daniel. That only becomes clear to me now that I start to wonder what was going on inside him in the years when we were growing up together— now that I ask myself how it was possible that he was forced into isolation the way he was, what it was that seemed so hopeless to him, whether he could have given a precise name to it. I don't know, and I expect some things have been blurred or rearranged by time, wound about with strands of memories that refuse to mesh.

Into this gap of not-knowing I sometimes insert fantasies of a happier Daniel, one who had a hobby I didn't know about—a small, enchanted garden with flowers and plants that were no longer needed at his parents' nursery. I see him cycling to this secret garden after school or work—or else I see him with a girlfriend, a girl who liked his square shoulders and green eyes, who would have sat on the stones by the river with him, watching the ships leave for the sea. I imagine a Daniel who loved the way you were supposed to love back then; I imagine that all my suspicions were wrong. Maybe he just kept his girl-friend a secret, or she came from another part of town. Maybe that's why we never saw him with a girl.

I piece this other Daniel together in my imagination because I wish I'd known more back then, wish I knew more today, wish he'd had more happiness in that short life of his—or more than I can imagine, anyway, given the time we spent together. It wasn't a very happy or carefree time.

Sometimes, though rarely, I imagine less pleasant things into that gap. I see him drifting off the rails, getting involved in dodgy deals. I see him unable to find his way back after dealing a bit of grass, doing a bit of shoplifting or winning a nasty fight. I see him loitering at truck stops, in strip bars, in the toilets where the rent boys hang out. These fantasies don't come so easily; they don't gel with the real Daniel of my childhood; they make no sense. But at least they'd provide an explanation for his death other than despair over his lonely desire.

—

He appeared in our lives as a deliveryman. One day there he was, standing on our doorstep with a paper bag of fresh rolls. It was a sensation. We never had fresh rolls in the morning. Fruit and veg were fresh, but bread and rolls came sliced in a plastic bag or heated up from the freezer. He called himself 'Gilbert' and really, that name, breathed with a hint of Frenchness, should have aroused everyone's suspicions. But the rolls were good and Gilbert was always punctual, always cheerful and friendly, and before long he was offering to drop in and mow the lawn too, or help out in some other way.

Gilbert was in his late twenties or early thirties, tall and athletic with rather pasty skin that showed up the dark hairs on his body. His black hair with a side parting always bobbed up and down slightly when he bounced up to our front door from the garden gate. He was on his bike from six in the morning, when the baker's opened, riding all over town to deliver his rolls.

Before long he was in and out of all the houses where young people of his preferred age were to be found, and he soon gained the parents' trust and the children's interest. I'd never heard the word 'paedophile'; I suspect that my parents hadn't either. I'm not sure they knew there was such a thing—adults who manipulated and abused children. If they did, sexuality remained dim and far off to them, though it was in fact real and close, and had been for some time. In adults and young people alike, lust and desire were blanked out, untouched by words, only circumscribed, as if with a pair of compasses whose centre was fixed, and which could only draw ever larger circles, without touching the space inside.

I knew Schubert's setting of Goethe's ballad *The Erl King* in Dietrich Fischer-Dieskau's recording and liked the muted sense of drama with which the terrible story was intoned. I had listened to it countless times at home, but had always heard in it the tale of a fearful father who is afraid for the life of his sick son, rather than that of a panicking child being harassed by an adult.

I don't know whether it was my upbringing, the place where we grew up or my own unconcern, but back then there were hardly any zones of fear. There were no forbidden spaces in the outside world, no areas we were warned of, no streets we were told to avoid. We disappeared to school in the mornings and into the woods at the weekend, we walked along the river or through the streets; we hung around and nobody worried about us.

We knew, of course, not to get into strangers' cars— not to let strangers cajole us into going with them. We saw the pictures of the Baader-Meinhof gang on the wanted posters on the station and in the post office, and every week *Case Number XY...Unsolved*, the German *Crimestoppers* or *Crimewatch*, spread fear and horror with its true-life cases. But sexual abuse and paedophilia weren't dangers that were addressed or mentioned at school. Why any stranger would want to bundle us into his car, and what would happen to us if we got in, was passed over in silence. A more head-on approach would have meant spelling out that young people were potential objects of lust—that our bodies were potentially desirable. The idea that we might have had desires of our own was completely unimaginable.

In a world in which sexuality is taboo, and lust features as an ambivalent and troubling void, there can be no negotiation over different forms of lust. When desire itself is discredited, it is no longer possible to distinguish between different kinds of desire. Paradoxically, the negation of lust leads to the dissolution of its boundaries. Only when desire is figured as lust—as something that has to do with unconditional want—can there be boundaries; only then does it become possible to demarcate the kind of sexuality that has nothing to do with want and offends against individuals' desires and fantasies.

That is the crux of the conflict surrounding the systematic abuse of children in Catholic institutions in Ireland, Germany and the United States, but it is also the crux of sexual violence and of the abuse of women and homosexuals in those Muslim societies where lust and desire are just as suppressed as female or homosexual subjectivity. When lust as such is forbidden, *every* form of desire becomes transgressive, making it impossible to distinguish between different kinds of transgression. If what you yourself want is deemed unthinkable, that means, regrettably, that you lose sight of what others— women or children—might want. Or, of course, what they don't want.

In a sexually repressive world, whether Muslim

or Catholic, where people are prevented from discovering their own lust, puberty is aborted or gets stuck in a time loop, and adult men remain in a state of pre-desire, wrapped in a cocoon of acquired shame. As a result, their forbidden lust can, if at all, only be expressed in combination with guilt—that explains why it is often released violently. A man's shame at his own desire is converted into contempt for the object that arouses the forbidden lust. What is vented on the object of lust is not in fact anger at the female body or the boy's body, but anger at the man's own misunderstood desire.

Abuse and sexual violence in liberal Protestant institutions such as the Odenwald School seem to point to the reverse conflict: when hierarchy and dependence are rejected on principle, and the discourse of 'reform pedagogy' denies all real power relations, then the boundaries between pupils and teachers, young people and adults, are no longer clearly discernible and the distinction is blurred between conscious symmetrical desire and the asymmetrical exploitation and abuse of the timid and naïve longing for recognition from a revered teacher. In such cases the offenders deny their own acts because they deny the unequal relations of power and force, romanticising the asymmetry of abuse and rape as the symmetry of desire.

Anyone who doesn't know what's happening to them in puberty, or what they're in for, will desire vaguely, with no particular object, except to be wanted by adults—by a choirmaster or a teacher. Anyone who grows up in a milieu where teachers officially deny their position of power, and unofficially exploit it, will find no basis in this imagined equality and similarity for resisting abuse and violence.[5]

You darling child, come with me, do!
Such lovely games I'll play with you.
The shore is covered in colourful flowers,
My mother has hundreds of golden gowns.

My father, my father, but can't you hear
What Erl King's whispering in my ear?
Hush, my child, hush, my love,
It's only the wind in the leaves above.[6]

Gilbert was soon appearing daily. He became as much a part of our world as the evening news and his presence was so discreet and so normal that people stopped asking what he was actually doing in our lives. He was as familiar as a plant. He helped out with repairs, did odd jobs; he was always around. And one day he invited us to drop in on him some time. Jakob, Markus, Thomas and I walked through the park to Gilbert's place not long after. As usual, I didn't even notice that I was the only girl in a band of boys. Gilbert lived on the slopes of a hill in a squat basement flat with a small door opening onto a garden that looked down into the valley. He had a record player that surely couldn't have been paid for out of a delivery-man's wages, but more importantly he had an impressive record collection, and so we lolled around on his mattress sofas, listening to David Bowie's 'Teenage Wildlife' and 'It's No Game'. Annoyingly, they were on two sides of the same record, so that we had to keep turning it over. The boys would flip it over before we reached the end of Side A, as soon as we'd had 'Ashes to Ashes'—and later even before it started.

We were soon regulars at Gilbert's place in the after-noons. There was nothing dodgy about that; it was simply an unwritten space, an in-between world. Gilbert's flat was exactly halfway between school and home, but there was also something fuzzy and indeterminate about Gilbert himself that attracted us; he was in between our parents' generation and our own, grown up and yet youthful, and he didn't expect anything of us—or at least that's what we thought. He didn't make us feel the pressure of authori-tarian conventions or the norms of childhood. Whereas at home and school we usually had to act more like children than we felt, at Gilbert's we could feel more grown up than we were.

We spent hours listening to music in this low-lying studio flat. Gilbert didn't make a big thing of it; he didn't badger us or ask questions. We could be the way we wanted there and that was appealing. It became something of a habit, that place that was defined more by what it wasn't than by what it was. As long as we were there, we could simply *be*, and Gilbert *was* with us. The discrepancies in our experience and knowledge gradually faded and we grew more and more alike. Any signs that might have highlighted the age difference were overwritten by our sense of fellowship; like beings without a history, we adapted ourselves—or he did. Over time Gilbert became one of us and we moved about that adult space as if it belonged to us. Jakob was given a key so that we could, if we felt like it, get into the flat even when Gilbert wasn't around. That didn't seem strange to us. Gilbert would join us in the course of the afternoon, with no mention of how he'd spent his day, and his presence would merge with ours, as if by osmosis.

Will you go with me, my fine boy?

One day a friend of Gilbert turned up—Malcolm, a British artist, who must have been twenty years older than Gilbert and was always elegantly dressed in English tweed jackets—a kind of diminutive Sherlock Holmes. Such a screaming cliché of an English homosexual seems absurd to us today. It must have been so obvious—the general aesthetics, the whole camp act, the clothes, the gestures, the little moustache he was always fingering. All the codes of gay comportment were clearly visible, and yet no one saw Malcolm as gay. He offered to give

75

us drawing lessons for a fee and our parents agreed; it must have seemed better to them than having us roam the streets. Suddenly, the open-ended afternoons had structure; with Malcolm there was work to be done. We no longer sat around idle, but drew and rubbed out and redrew, following instructions, like at school. Gilbert had moved by then, into a smaller but lighter flat on the river. We used to walk sand into his rooms; sometimes he'd take off our shoes because of this, sometimes he'd wash the sand from our bare feet.

If it hadn't been for Malcolm and his strange drawing classes, I too might have drifted into an ambivalent mixture of lust and repulsion, curiosity and aversion— or maybe I'd have been cast out by Gilbert at an earlier stage because I was the wrong sex, and because my body, however youthful and androgynous, didn't turn him on. In the end, it was quite simply my lack of artistic talent that forced me out of the group. I was so abysmal at drawing that I soon lost interest and just as I had previously been attracted by the indefinable nature of those afternoons in Gilbert's flat, I was suddenly disturbed by the order that now emerged, the aesthetic specifications we were expected to meet in our work—there they were again, those norms you were supposed to acquire.

I love you, your nice shape's a lure.
And if you're not willing, I'll have to use force!

It must have been one of the first nights they spent there, a whole group of them. It hadn't surprised them that Gilbert wanted to sleep in the room with them—he was one of them, after all; we'd all thought that, and he'd probably even thought it himself; he'd probably regarded himself as a young person, just like us. The illusion wasn't broken until Gilbert put his hand on the crotch of one of those boys half his age and began to stroke his penis.

I don't know whether it was Gilbert's whimpering moans and clumsy fumbling (which I only found out about years after the event) or whether it was his fear of discovery or simply the fact that he didn't threaten to use force—but his sexual overtures precipitated the break-up of the group; where, until then, there had been equality and similarity, there was now division. Gilbert wasn't one of us; he was different. The scene had revealed him in all his anguished lust; none of the boys desired him and any initial curiosity at the unexpected physical contact soon gave way to disgust. We may have been inexperienced back then, but the power of the older man who had hoped to take advantage of that inexperience quickly tipped over into the powerlessness of one who had thrown himself on the mercy of a group of boys secure in their social position. The class instinct of the sons of the bourgeoisie flared up; the moment Gilbert dared touch a suburban kid's penis, resentment was aroused towards a man who wasn't one of them—*couldn't* be one of them.

In Gilbert, the naked, feverishly aroused Gilbert, they saw once again the deliveryman, the odd-job man who had mown their parents' lawns, and it was this Gilbert whose sexual endeavours they rejected. No charges were brought against him; none of the boys reported the incident, either to their parents or to school; he was merely ridiculed and then ignored. In this display of noli-me-tangere these young people, who just about knew how to masturbate but hadn't yet slept with a girlfriend or boyfriend, brought their superiority to bear against an adult who had left his cover. For those young middle-class machos, that was harder to forgive than the fact that he'd touched them.

What, I wonder, would have happened in a different milieu? Would young people without the social conceit of those middle-class kids have known how to resist the advances of an older man? It was the arrogance of their class, their practised condescension that proved protective to these boys because it gave them another, more powerful inequity to pit against the psychological inequity of the adult–child relationship.

—

Anyone looking at old issues of the German teen magazine *Bravo*[7] today will wonder how we children of the seventies and eighties, straight or queer, were ever sexualised at all. It certainly wasn't thanks to the visual language and aesthetic style of the seventies pop icons. Of course, back then, the *Bravo* 'star cut' of the Village People was something of a sensation—a fifty-three-piece puzzle that could be stuck together to make a life-size poster of the superstar group, the oiled body of 'Felipe the Indian' (crouched in the foreground to show off his tensed thigh muscles) shining out at you more than lasciviously. But those milky prints of blurred photographs showing chubby young people in prudish white underwear were so sweaty and bland that I find it hard to believe how excited we were by them.

Every week we'd pounce greedily on the *Bravo* picture stories as if they were porn films in comic format, following in flustered excitement the episodes that were always over too soon—always ending when the couple were pressed up against one another at last, somewhere in a cellar or on a meadow—and always, I seem to remember, when the boy pushed his hand under the girl's bra or down her knickers, but never when the girl pushed her hand down the boy's pants. *Bravo* stopped, like a torn film, just before our lust could be properly released.

No wonder, then, that I had my first orgasm fully clothed and standing up, when Dirk and I (Dirk was the drummer of The Inmates, the school band at another local school) unexpectedly threw ourselves at each other at a party at his house. It was as if I wanted to see one of those *Bravo* stories through to the end at last—although still within the logic of the story, without sex and without nudity. We stood there, penetrating one another without penetration. To be honest, it was unfair and asymmetrical. My arousal was mounting; he was already hard enough for me to be able to rub myself against him feverishly and we were both far too surprised to think of getting undressed and having sex. Perhaps if we had, everything would have melted away; perhaps it was the chance, improvised, almost unwanted nature of the encounter that appealed. I'd never been interested in Dirk, who was neither particularly attractive nor properly cool; he possessed only this wildly attractive lack of interest in me that made it possible for me to desire him, for me to initiate things, and so we pressed up against one another and suddenly all the pent-up lust that for years had been prematurely interrupted in those picture stories, was released in a long tremor, my first orgasm, ultimately an act of exploitation vis-à-vis Dirk, because no sooner was I satisfied than I went home feeling happy and confused about what had happened—about the force that had come over me, taken me apart and put me back together again more or less clumsily—leaving him standing heated and aroused in the hall of his terraced house.

I don't suppose that's quite what *Bravo* intended with its photo romances. The idea was to offer sensitive enlightenment to a generation whose parents didn't know how to talk about sex, forcing them to turn to *Bravo*'s weekly advice column with their questions. Daniel and

I were teenagers in the age of agony uncle Dr Martin Goldstein, alias Dr Sommer or Dr Korff, who, unlike his infamous female predecessor, was at least capable of separating sex from morality and didn't reject homosexuality on principle.[8]

In 1972, two articles in *Bravo*, intended to inform readers about homosexual practices as part of 'The New Series About Love Without Fear', were put on the Index at the request of the Bavarian State Ministry of Labour and Social Affairs. The Federal Review Board for Publications Harmful to Young Persons had consulted various opinions and testimonials before putting both issues on the Index in October 1972 despite expert recommendation, because it regarded 'the presentation of sexual acts between girls (Issue 6) and between boys (Issue 7) as "the disintegration of sexuality in the overall social character" and thus as "conceptually confusing from a socio-ethical point of view".'[9]

In his defence of the 'enlightening reportages' written under the pseudonym of Dr Korff, Goldstein argued that the texts were purely informative—that far from inciting homoerotic practices, their aim was merely to present a phenomenon that he himself regarded as a 'prolonged homoerotic phase' in many young people. It is noteworthy that Goldstein explicitly rejected the demonisation of homosexuality prevalent at the time by refusing to criminalise it: 'It would be nonsense to forbid or taint the homosexual energies that are present in all people.'[10]

We knew nothing of this lawsuit, nothing of the political culture of censure, but our imagination, stimulated or guided by the *Bravo* romances, was hemmed about by constraints. Week after week, questions about homosexuality featured in the readers' letters ('He suddenly reached into my sleeping bag when we were camping'; 'I am troubled by a boy') and although the feelings described in these letters were, with some sensitivity, declared normal—Dr Sommer and Dr Korff tried to rid our generation of the fear that homosexuals were perverse or sick—they were also relativised; the desire for one's own sex was reduced to a passing phase, a somnambulistic confusion, a kind of experiment with a single possible outcome—heterosexuality.

A typical example: 'My problem,' writes a thirteen-year-old boy, 'is that I'm gay. That may not sound so bad, but the real problem is this: I don't actually want to be gay. When I see a naked boy I get a hard penis and want to masturbate. But I'd like to get a hard penis when I see naked girls.' The boy asks whether he should consult his doctor, whether he can have medical treatment. 'Is there any help for me?'

Dr Sommer's reply is spectacular: 'Just because you get a hard penis when you see a naked boy, you think you're gay...'[11]

You couldn't make it up. Rather than allaying the

boy's fear of his desire, Dr Sommer explains it away. I suppose we should be grateful that the answer wasn't: 'How can you be aroused when you see a naked boy?' I suppose it was a pedagogical advance that the boy wasn't told he was a threat to public order with his hard-on.

In our secondary-school days, a story was printed under the title 'How Does a Boy Know He's Gay?', in which Dr Korff promises to address 'the most intimate questions'. We hear about 'Frank' who is feeling bored at a party one day until 'Albrecht' sits down next to him, touches him and strokes him, provoking 'Frank' to wonder timidly whether 'Albrecht' might be gay. In his reply, Dr Korff pronounces 'Frank' a sensitive, serious boy, who isn't keen on silly jokes about girls and enjoys being touched by 'Albrecht'—'but that has nothing to do with being gay'.

I can't recall that anything in *Bravo* ever had to do with being gay. Homoerotic practices existed and were not—which was something—regarded as abnormal, but homosexual lust was never allowed to acquire such depth or power that it might have assumed existential proportions, influencing or changing your life.

I'd have liked to produce a reverse *Bravo*, one in which all erotic discoveries were initiated by the girls, an issue where she put her hand in his pants, pushed him passionately against an oven door (I'd have stopped there, out of sheer spite), or one where all the stories were homosexual and the advice column was full of desperate letters from boys who got a hard-on at the sight of a girl and turned in concern to Dr Sommer: 'Am I sick? Can it be treated?' The reply would be reassuring: 'Why do you think you're heterosexual,' Dr Sommer would ask, 'just because you get a hard-on at the sight of a girl?' Besides, heterosexual desire was nothing unusual; it was a phase plenty of adolescents went through; it would pass.

I don't remember specific texts from the *Bravo* of my youth. But I do remember that beside the faintly sweaty atmosphere of lust, *Bravo* also frequently spread a fear of unwanted 'seduction': pupils could be 'seduced' by their (female) teachers, hitchhiking boys by lorry drivers, girls by other girls—I seem to recall that most articles about unwelcome advances or eroticism were connected with homosexual lust; paedophilia, whether intentionally or not, was coupled with homosexuality, and I had a lasting idea that homoeroticism had something to do with coercion.

This blurred with other topics and texts, always remaining peripheral—but while *Bravo* opened up certain taboo zones, there were other areas whose boundaries it only drew more sharply.

—

Growing up seemed to come with bad smells. Not that I'd been banished from the woods; I still roamed around there. But the world could no longer be discovered on foot like in the first years of secondary school. All my early explorations took me over sandy terrain—along the riverbank, off the paths in the woods, or on the school cinder pitch where we played football. Then at some point the impromptu football games were replaced by organised matches at the handball club and weekly training in the cold and sweaty army gym in a remote barracks. Oddly enough, that appears to have been quite common. Our school's old gym belonged to the local police station. Sport still seemed to be topographically rooted in the police and military world of physical training—although our progressive left-wing teachers and coaches knew how to undermine this association.

Our teenage territory was widened, geographically, by the weekend matches that had us travelling back and forth on the underground to sports halls in far-flung parts of town. The whole team would meet outside the newly opened Burger King at our local station and we'd set off together. On the way back, we'd all go and have a burger, whether we'd won or lost.

At the same time, the world began to expand socially, because almost all the girls on the handball team came from other schools. Grammar-school girls like me were in the minority, and we were late developers, 'half ripe'. All the girls on my team were rather sturdier than me, not to mention bigger breasted. They came from the same part of town, but from a different world. We lived only a few streets away from each other, but we'd never met; we knew nothing of each other.

As well as being split into different social zones, our world was divided according to a hierarchy of educational institutions. Grammar-school pupils and pupils from the local comprehensive didn't meet; there was no overlap, and conscientious grammar-school parents made sure at an early stage that the mechanics of distinction were in full working order. That was the unspoken reason for the tennis lessons, ballet classes and riding teachers they organised; these extracurricular activities were an investment in maintaining class privilege. What looked like an innocent recreation or hobby only served to reproduce a milieu. If you learnt an expensive individual sport, your chances of having to mix with children from a different background were lower—it was as simple as that. But the handball team brought together two worlds that were kept neatly separate during the school day and rarely met in everyday local life.

I don't know whether it was desire that drove me to take up handball or, if it was desire, what kind it was. I don't know whether it was simply that the world of handball seemed to me less regimented and I was attracted by the relative freedom from norms, or whether I liked the girls, who were feminine in a way so completely different from what was acceptable among the girls I knew. Neither motive was one I could have talked about.

I felt at ease there. Everything, including the sport itself, seemed rougher, more physical, more direct. I liked the simplicity of the game. I preferred the leather weight of the ball to the fluffy lightness of a lurid yellow tennis ball. There were no club houses, no wood-panelled bars where cliquey families got together; there was just handball. The only thing that counted was how I played. And to begin with, I played badly.

I was slightly younger than the others, and smaller. That wasn't the case at school, where we were all the same age and I was one of the keenly athletic children, at least as far as any kind of ball game went. There was a well-established and unspoken hierarchy in our class of social, aesthetic and athletic criteria which was constantly reinforced in humiliating rituals: picking teams or handing out birthday-party invitations.

If you were sporty like me you could avoid ridicule and mockery, even over a period of many years, because we were all much of a muchness age-wise, and the variations in puberty weren't significant enough to have any great effect on the hierarchy. At the handball club things were different. I may not have been teased during my first year on the team, when all the others were bigger than me, but I wasn't shown any respect either. I had to wait an entire season—until the older players had left to join the next team up—to be taken seriously, and it took me as long to understand how humiliating it felt to be trapped, helpless, on the margins of a group.

Did I notice back then that I desired in a different way? Would it have been possible to combine the discovery of desire with the discovery that I desired slightly differently from the others? How do we discover desire anyway? Is there an inner core of lust clamouring to express itself, searching for a form? Does desire emerge and take shape, growing less vague and more precise in its wants, regardless of what happens to us? Or is it only in and through experience that desire is formed? Does our imagination need to know what is possible or can it fuel itself?

Did I start to play handball because I was attracted by the other girls' social background? Or did I only begin to like that world once the sport had made it familiar to me? Whatever it was that made me feel at ease, was it there all along, or did the sense of belonging develop with experience?

I'm not interested in why I'm homosexual—whether my desire is considered genetically predetermined or socially conditioned. What relevance could it have? What difference does it make? I'm interested in how desire emerges—in me, but also in others—how I became aware of it, how it developed, found a language, found expression in me and for me—and how that language grew, its vocabulary constantly expanding, its syntax increasingly complex, allowing me to express myself more precisely, more tenderly, more radically.

Looking back, we often interpret the past in relation to the present, giving our lives a coherence that makes it seem logical that we have turned out the way we have. Intellectuals allegedly devoured Kafka and Spinoza even as small children; talk-show hosts did take-offs of TV shows as teenagers; politicians displayed signs of leadership from the cradle—and homosexuals had to be different right from the start: football-mad girls or dancing boys.

Stereotyped clichés don't only shut people out; they also shut them in and restrain them. Because any deviation from the norm requires a plausible explanation, a reason, a plot free from ambivalence and contradiction, the stories we tell about the way people live rely on categories that squeeze everybody—but perhaps minorities in particular—into linear, homogeneous plots. We tend to iron out stories of desire, to make linear developments of them after the fact, depriving lust of all its lustful ambiguity. In hindsight my handball playing seems to fit into the scheme of things better than my love of classical music. And from an outside perspective, it is easy to blot out the fact that I fell in love with men all through those early years—happily in love, what's more.

—

The images slip. It's like finding sequences of photos from different occasions or holidays on the same negative strip—pictures taken at different times. That used to happen to me sometimes, when I'd left the film in my camera for so long that I'd forgotten what was on it by the time I got round to developing it. Not until the strip was drying in the darkroom would all those moments I'd forgotten or thought I'd lost forever suddenly re-emerge, and unconnected experiences would appear side by side on the film roll, making it possible to think one set of pictures together with a much later set.

In the same way, pictures of the past, of Daniel or me, shift and link up with pictures from the present. I look back and forth from one time or place to another—from the town where we grew up to the landscapes I travel through today, from our desire back then, under its layer of silence, to others' similarly silenced desire today—and in the spaces between those images, I write.

A friend had recommended an interpreter, a young student; his English, she said, was excellent, and she'd known the family for ages—as if that mattered to me. It wasn't, after all, as if I wanted his grandmother to translate Arabic interviews into English for me, but it would presumably boost our security, should we run into danger—being in touch with a well-known family would mean having a circle of allies at our disposal.

And now here he was. Ibrahim stood before us and we stared at this apparition, unable to believe what we were seeing, as if he were a mirage that might fade to a shimmering blur before our eyes. Ibrahim was wearing jeans, a radiant white puffer jacket and a pair of oversized sunglasses such as George Michael might have worn in the eighties. He invited us to drink tea with him in the hotel where we'd arranged to meet, sitting down gingerly on the edge of a chair, as if he expected the seat to be taken away from him at any moment.

It was clear from Ibrahim's first words of greeting, from his first answers to our questions—was he available all day long? Did he mind translating interviews with people who supported both Hamas and Fatah, as well as supporters of each group? As soon as he began to speak, in an excited voice and unexcited and impeccable English, something that shouldn't have been clear was clear: that Ibrahim was gay—a gay man in Gaza.

Working with Ibrahim was wonderful; he was a sensitive person and a fine interpreter with a keen feeling for the different languages and forms of expression used by the people we talked to—from the family man whose daughter had been killed by Israeli tank shelling to the militant Islamic jihad supporter who targeted Israeli residents of Ashdod by planting rockets in strangers' gardens and detonating them with a time fuse; from timid nurses to lusty wedding musicians. Day and night Ibrahim was with us and as he moved between the various social groups and lines of conflict of his own society, explaining them to us, in his slightly overexcited way, we had the impression he wasn't part of this society.

How were we to broach the subject? How could we ask him? Everything about him must create a sensation in this region: his clothes, his gestures, his gentle manner. Ibrahim invoked cultural codes we weren't sure he knew. In Gaza there are no public theatres, no cinemas, no concerts; there is little public music except at weddings and funerals. The pirated DVDs with sun-bleached covers you see hawked on the market in Gaza City are all too often American war films. There's nothing on television except Syrian and Turkish soaps, and even they are constantly interrupted because electricity in Gaza works in eight-hour shifts. After that, everything is out of action for eight hours and no one has electricity unless they can afford a generator. If girls or young women want to meet up with men before getting married, they're not allowed out alone, but have to have a sister or cousin to chaperone them. This means that a lot of clandestine couples go to internet cafés to sit next to each other at separate computers and chat. It's the only way they have of getting to know one another, of talking or flirting.[12]

Was it possible that Ibrahim wasn't aware of the impression he created? How was he to know, after all? But mustn't he, if nothing else, notice that he looked different and acted differently from the other young men around him? How had it come about? Didn't he know how gay he acted? But was he even gay? How could we be so sure? Weren't we making hackneyed imputations, relying on clichés? Just because somebody moves like Albin in *La Cage aux Folles*, it doesn't have to mean he's gay. And wasn't it rather reckless of us simply to transfer our own aesthetic codes—all those signals that are constantly being undermined and renegotiated, even in the West? Why were we applying them here in Gaza so unscrupulously, so flatfootedly?

The pictures shift.

Was I so different from Ibrahim when I was growing up? Were things perhaps more obvious to others than they were to me? Did I perhaps seem like a typical tomboy to the others? Didn't I, too, tick all the boxes? Wasn't I, too, permanently at odds with what was expected of a girl of my age? Wasn't I constantly rebellious and out of joint? Isn't that one reason I felt so comfortable playing handball?

How similar was my ignorance back then to Ibrahim's today in the Gaza Strip?

The difference was that my homosexuality—conscious or unconscious, lived or not—didn't put me at risk. Homosexuality in Gaza, on the other hand, is regarded as a sin, an offence, and the only way of living safely as a gay person in Gaza is to live your homosexuality in secret.[13] Because the borders are closed, you can't simply flee the Strip unless you possess a foreign passport or are granted rare permission to leave by the Israelis (for urgent hospital treatment, for example, or sometimes to study). Exile for homosexual Palestinians in Gaza is, of necessity, inner exile.

Whether or not Ibrahim was aware of his appearance, it was risky. Or was it possible that we were the only ones who saw it? Was the taboo a victim of its own effectiveness? Had homosexuality been suppressed to such an extent that Hamas didn't even recognise a gay man when he was standing right in front of them? If you're not allowed to talk about homosexuality, you're not allowed to talk about what constitutes it either.

Curiously enough, the question of Ibrahim's sexuality was made more difficult by the fact that homosexual practices in Gaza, as in other repressive societies, Muslim and non-Muslim, are by no means rare—as a substitute for forbidden premarital sex with women. Because heterosexual sex before or outside marriage is impossible, men often practise homosexual sex tacitly, without either man thinking or being permitted to think the other is gay. Thus one form of taboo sex facilitates another.

Should we warn him? Should we tell him what impression he created? Our first trip came to an end and we said nothing. If he really had no idea about his desire, what confusion might a simple question cause? What might it spark off in him? We'd go home and leave him alone with a lead he wouldn't be able to follow up in Gaza without putting his life at risk. Besides, any question or conversation about sexuality seemed to me too intimate. It wasn't only that I didn't know Ibrahim well enough to ask him about his desire; it also seemed altogether shameless to broach a topic that nobody here talked about.

Still, Ibrahim did feel confident enough to ask a favour of us: would we take a present to a friend on the West Bank? The Gaza Strip was still sealed off; Ibrahim was trapped in those forty-two kilometres. He wasn't allowed through the high-security terminal of Eretz, the only border crossing to Israel. And so he gave us a small mug with a Palestinian text and a T-shirt for 'a friend' who lived in Ramallah. That could have meant anything but, ashamed that we were permitted to leave the territory while he could only long for it, we were glad to take the parcel for him. ('Do you have anything in your luggage given to you by strangers—a gift, perhaps?' is the question routinely asked by Israeli border guards. No, we didn't.)

On our second trip to Gaza, we met Ibrahim again. And again we felt the urge to talk to him. A few days into our stay—we were in a taxi and Ibrahim, as usual, was leaning round to us from the front seat—I asked whether there were homosexuals in the Gaza Strip. I tried to make it sound as casual as possible, no big deal, just another question from a curious journalist, like when I asked about the material used for the strings of the *oud*, an Arabian lute, or the work of traditional marriage brokers. Ibrahim flinched slightly, and lowering his voice, as if the driver might understand English, he said tonelessly:

strange, a Dutch journalist had asked him that just the other day; there was an international NGO that dealt with such cases, but he didn't know precise details. That was it. No mention of his own situation—not a hint that he knew how other people in Gaza lived their desire. Nothing.

Perhaps we were wrong?

There was another unforgettable scene on this second trip. We had asked Ibrahim to arrange for us to meet up with some young women students who could tell us about their lives—preferably a small group, so that they'd find it easier to talk. We wanted to find out how young women in Gaza envisage their lives before others make decisions for them and marry them off. Ibrahim said it was no trouble—he'd ask some friends—and soon we were sitting with six young women between nineteen and twenty-three, all students, all veiled except one who had a Spanish passport and would soon be leaving the territory. They spoke frankly and cheerfully about themselves and the lives they lived in the gaps and crevices of a system that hemmed them in on all sides. They told us they could only ever go out in a group and weren't allowed to see boys alone; meetings with young men were hedged about by norms and sanctions, and only tolerated when they had a functional purpose—when there were prospects of marriage. Such was the static horizon of all female lives in Gaza.

They told us these things and Ibrahim sat there with us. After a while I asked how they could be friends with Ibrahim—he was a man, after all. The young women laughed as if I'd asked a particularly daft question. They didn't hesitate for a second with the answer: Ibrahim? Yes, Ibrahim was something different. That wasn't a problem.

What exactly that 'something different' was, remained unspoken.

For the rest of our trip, we didn't touch on the subject again. During the day we researched our respective stories, travelling all over the Gaza Strip, from the refugee camps in the north to the illegal tunnels that lead to Egypt, and returning to the hotel in the late evening when we'd sit on the terrace over sweet tea with mint, and talk about what we'd seen and heard. Sometimes we also talked about our life outside, beyond the borders of the Gaza Strip.

On one of these evenings I told Ibrahim I was homosexual. Ibrahim accepted this piece of information as if I'd said I loved rap; he was pleased to find out something about me, but he didn't pursue the subject. He didn't ask what it was like to love a woman, or whether homosexuality was a threat where I lived.

Our third and last trip was special. The Israeli army had begun a military offensive in Gaza in response to the regular rocket attacks—a further escalation in the circle of violence. For more than two weeks we tried to enter Gaza from Israel while the war was still underway, but the entire international press was banned from passing the border post of Eretz and had to wait until the last Israeli tank had left the Gaza strip. We didn't get to Gaza until everything was over.

Ibrahim had survived. He was unshaven and spoke even more quickly than usual. Some of what he said made no sense. His sentences were in tatters; words hung loose like threads and weren't picked up until later. He spoke more to himself than to us, as if he had to put all the horrors of war into some kind of order in his own mind before reporting on them to anyone else. He was clearly pleased to see us and said so several times, almost as soon as we got in the car just across the border, where he picked us up as usual.

He wanted to show us the damage wreaked by the war; he was keen for us to research everything thoroughly—in the hospitals and in the refugee camp of Jabalia—but first we must have some chai with mint. Ibrahim and I sat there alone, just the two of us; he was wearing the white puffer jacket he always wore and a scarf, and he looked raw and naked, as if the war had stripped the skin from his body, exposing the flesh—and as we were sitting there, he suddenly said: 'I'm gay.'

He said it out of the blue, unprompted, without explaining when he'd discovered or why he suddenly felt the urge to tell me. He didn't have to. I could imagine what he'd seen in the last days of the war—how trivial everything had come to seem; how arbitrary, random and excruciating dying, and how absurd survival, as if life hardly mattered. I could imagine him, with the time lag typical in such cases, learning to be afraid; that icy fear, cold as the sweat that soaks your shirt, only ever sets in once the danger's over. I could imagine, because I had seen it in countless other wars, more things dying every day—first neighbours and acquaintances, then the familiar surroundings: the buildings whose storeys come crashing down on top of one another and stick together like the sponge and cream of a layer cake, with no space in between; the orange groves Ibrahim used to walk through—gone, shot to pieces, bombed, torn up by tanks, because, so the military logic goes, orange and olive trees might be hiding missile-launching pads; and now, where there were once green and orange landscapes, there were only black, bony roots sticking up out of burnt-out groves. I could imagine all the children he had distracted from their pain as they watched their own skin fall off in shreds when they had their dressings changed in hospital. I could imagine the deafening noise of the air raids, because what the other survivors talked about more than anything, now that it was over, was how unbelievably quiet it was.

What difference did it make if he came out now?

'I'm gay,' said Ibrahim again, as if he wanted to hear what it sounded like. 'I know, Ibrahim,' I said. He turned his tired eyes on me in astonishment. He seemed to want to ask how another person could know something he hadn't known himself, but he said nothing. Sitting right on the edge of the chair like at our first meeting, he said: 'I've never told anyone before.'

He'd been captured by Hamas in the middle of the war and interrogated. It wasn't clear what Hamas knew, whether it was actually Hamas at all or what exactly Ibrahim was being accused of. Tactical vagueness is one of the tools of the totalitarian regime; there is method in those hazy white patches of language that help to generate a diffuse fear; they form the rhetorical repertoire of violence. Torturers use fuzzy allegations and charges to spread terror; it's not so easy to defend yourself against vagueness. Ibrahim was accused of 'collaborating with the Israeli enemy'—that was the standard formulation. He had aroused suspicion: whether because of his otherness, his political views, his work with international journalists or his manner, remained hazy. The only thing that wasn't hazy was the fear it had left in him.

Ibrahim is not called Ibrahim. He has now fled Gaza for a European country that was willing to issue him with the papers he required to exit the territory legally. For a year he was penned up with other refugees from other parts of the world in a home for asylum seekers, waiting for a response to his request. His family in Gaza don't know why he fled. They know nothing about his sexual orientation; they have no idea that what is considered a crime in Gaza is the reason for his right to stay in Europe, and ultimately his asylum.

We still write to each other.

In the town where Ibrahim now lives, he recently went to a gay bar for the first time. I had assumed it would make him happy to see how natural that is, how easy. I'd thought he'd be glad to be able to express himself at last, without fear. I'd thought it would be nice for him to meet others, to discover that there is an entire community—that homosexuality doesn't have to mean a life of loneliness—that there are other forms of familiarity, community, home.

But Ibrahim was outraged. It was superficial, he said, indiscreet—the aggressive lust, the compliments the men made him, without even knowing him. He shuddered. Sure, it was freedom, and he was glad not to have to be ashamed of his homosexuality—but did that mean it had to be shameless? He sat there, a recognised refugee in Europe, free to live out his desire—but he hadn't shaken his loneliness. Happiness was within reach, but he didn't share in it.

He lives in the backroom of a shop with another newly arrived refugee. Sometimes, Ibrahim wrote to me recently, he'd like to talk to someone who knew both— Gaza and the person he was back then *and* this European metropolis and the life it offers homosexuals.

The change of place has brought with it a change of perspective on what Ibrahim sees as rejection, what he has to hide because it might be regarded as different or threatening. In the past, in Gaza, it was his homosexuality that marked him out as other; today, in Europe, it's his origins. As an Arab in Europe, religious or not so religious, Ibrahim, a Muslim homosexual, is coming to realise how arbitrary and varied others' perceptions of you can be—what they see you as, what they regard as objectionable.

—

The Statistical Yearbook of the Federal Republic of Germany for 1967, the year Daniel and I were born, records two thousand, two hundred and sixty-one men who were sentenced because of their homosexuality according to Paragraph 175 of the Criminal Code.[14]

I had to look that up. I belong to a generation that understands itself as queer and has been able to regard that as politically almost self-evident—but it never was self-evident and still isn't. If it were, Daniel's death wouldn't be so troubling to me; I wouldn't, all these years after our time together at school, still be pondering the conditions of possibility of desire, wondering why nobody wanted to see what was gnawing at Daniel, or perhaps—given that I wasn't even able to work out what was gnawing at me— why nobody was *able* to see it. Nor would I see so many people on my travels who are in the same predicament as we were in back then.

Another thing I had to read up on—reluctantly and a little incredulously—was what a ridiculously long time it took for criminal-law reforms on sexual offences to be implemented in West Germany. The political class opposed recommendations from psychologists and lawyers that homosexuality be legalised, and as a result, Nazi ideologies were perpetuated for decades.

Although the judicial system of the newly established Federal Republic of Germany had pledged to adopt laws from the Nazi era only insofar as they didn't go against the new constitution, the fascist tradition criminalising homosexuality as 'lewdness' was upheld when it came to the criminal law on sexual offences. In 1932 the Nazis had tightened up an 1872 paragraph, making the 'lascivious intent' of a man who desired another man a punishable offence. According to the revised paragraph, 'intercourse-like acts' (whatever they were) were no longer a necessary condition for punishment. Even contact was no longer necessary; it was enough for the general sense of shame to be offended. What exactly the 'general sense of shame' was and when it was offended remained subject to arbitrary definition. To justify the ban on homosexuality, Paragraph 175 drew on biopolitical rhetoric, combining ideological concepts of hygienic and moral purity, and demanding that the 'moral health of the nation' be protected from the 'epidemic propagation' of homosexuality.[15]

This notion of homosexuality as a 'pestilence', a 'disease' that can spread like an 'epidemic', has always surprised me. What fuels such a fantasy? How is 'contagion' supposed to occur? Through looking? (Anyone exposed to the gay gaze will become gay themselves?) Through droplet transference? Through sex?

Why should heterosexuals be so susceptible to seduction? And why did the legislators assume that it wouldn't stop at a glance or two, or a one-off try? Why should a one-time sexual experience turn into a full-blown reinvention of a person's sexuality? What does that say about the self-perception of heterosexuals? How insecure must their sense of sexual orientation be, if they believe it can be so swiftly infected by homosexuality? How vulnerable— to stick to the metaphor of sickness and health—does that make the heterosexual 'immune system'?

You only have to imagine the fantasy the other way round—that homosexuals were afraid of being exposed to the regard or lust of heterosexual people and left permanently marked, changed, deformed.

The fear of the 'epidemic' spread of homosexuality can be traced not only through the various arguments of the opponents to criminal-law reform who kept Paragraph 175 alive into the nineties; it is also tacitly present in laws like the 'don't ask, don't tell' policy in effect in the US army until 2010, which stipulated that although homosexual soldiers were allowed to serve in the US armed forces and go to war, they weren't allowed to *say* that they were homosexual. Implicit in this ruling was the idea that the speech act itself was dangerous—not the presence of gays in the army or their lived sexuality, but the idea that they might mention it—that what everyone suspected or knew might be given a name, might come true.

It's the opposite of the Rumpelstiltskin principle: whereas the imp in the fairytale loses his menace as soon as he can be named, the 'don't ask, don't tell' policy relies on ignorance, namelessness and not naming to provide reassurance and preserve the status quo. Sexuality in itself isn't alarming; only open and explicit sexuality. It is speaking the truth that creates unrest, while by the same token, lies and silence are regarded as stabilising.[16]

Together with the concept of the 'healthy body politic' inherited from the Nazis, the ideological fear of the spread of the 'disease' homosexuality lived on into the Federal Republic and was regularly reinforced in new rulings. The biopolitical terminology is still in evidence in a government draft of a penal code tabled under Konrad Adenauer in 1962: 'Where male homosexuality is concerned, it is, more than in other areas, the duty of the legal system to put up a dam to halt the spread of immoral practices which would, if they were to run rampant, pose a serious threat to the healthy and natural order of national life.'[17] The ease with which lawyers were still bandying about fascist terms is also evident in the following passage from the same bill: 'Wherever homosexual lewdness has run rampant and assumed significant proportions, the result has been the degeneration of the nation and the decline of its moral strength.'[18]

With the first criminal-law reform bill of 1969 under the grand coalition of Kurt Kiesinger, Paragraph 175 remained in force, but the total ban on homosexuality was lifted. When it came to 'lewdness between men', only so-called qualified cases had prison sentences imposed on them. These included homosexual sex with a man under the age of twenty-one (the so-called age of consent), the exploitation of dependence, and prostitution.[19]

During our secondary-school years, from 1977 to 1986, one thousand, five hundred and sixty-two men were sentenced under the toned-down version of Paragraph 175.

Lesbian women were never formally affected by the legislation.[20] When, in an attempt to repeal the law through high-court rulings, opponents of Paragraph 175 argued that besides being rooted in Nazi tradition, it also contravened the fundamental rights of Articles 2 and 3 of the German Constitution ('the free development of personality' and 'equal rights of men and women'), the Second Criminal Division of the Federal Court of Justice felt compelled in 1951 to provide an explanation as to why female homosexuality should be judged differently from male homosexuality: '[The non-penalisation] of so-called lesbian love [is] not in breach of the fundamental right to equality [...], because that right only prohibits the unequal treatment of that which is equal; it does not prohibit the treatment of different categories of persons according to their specific character'. The Court further referred to the 'natural differences between the sexes' which it saw as 'justifying the different legal treatment of the two types of homosexual lewdness'.[21]

I'm not saying I'd have been pleased if lesbian women had also been outlawed and had charges brought against them for the way they desired, but not to be perceived as lustfully threatening at all does perplex me from an analytical point of view. Why wasn't female homosexuality judged 'degenerate'? Why wasn't it perceived as a threat to the 'healthy body politic'? Why shouldn't female lust 'run rampant'?

When the Federal Constitutional Court confirmed the legitimacy of the original Paragraph 175 in 1957, it made the following statement on the question of the unequal treatment of male and female homosexuality: 'The sexual specificity of homosexual lewdness is evident both in the different physical forms of perpetration and in the different psychological behaviour involved in these acts and has, by virtue of these biological differences, a clear impact on the overall social image of this form of sexual activity.'[22]

Different physical 'forms of perpetration'? Is

perpetrating with lips and tongues and fingers and hands and whatever we use, breathlessly, to enter one another, touch one another, arouse one another—is that less harmful? Is it less epidemic or 'degenerate'? What is it about male biological differences that makes forms of perpetration between men so threatening? Anal intercourse? But that isn't the exclusive reserve of gay men; it's a sexual practice that can give women pleasure too. Maybe it's the misogynous fear of penetration, the notion that men can not only be fucked, but might even be aroused by it—is that what's considered subversive?

What kind of physical behaviour accompanies these *forms of perpetration*? (The more I write the words, the more wild my fantasies about what they might mean.) And what's the connection between physical forms of perpetration, psychological behaviour and social image? According to the Federal Constitutional Court: 'Male sexual behaviour is a great deal more likely than female sexual behaviour to fail to fulfil the cultural obligation to combine pleasure with a willingness to assume responsibility.'

Aside from the comical aspect of the biologistic and essentialist conviction that male sexuality is per se irresponsible and socially 'failed', this statement implicitly reinforces the stereotype of lustful, active male unrestraint and lustless female dutifulness.

Why wasn't female homosexuality banned?

Presumably because the Federal Constitutional Court was fundamentally unable to imagine female lust or desire, whether homosexual or heterosexual. The idea that women might have desires of their own, that there could be such a thing as female eroticism fuelled by a woman's lust and fantasy, was unimaginable. Female subjectivity, female Eros, distinct from male desire, freed from the bourgeois family's need for ties—none of that featured. 'Irresponsible', promiscuous female sexuality that wants only to express itself, to desire for the sake of desire, was so unthinkable that there was no need for taboos or bans.

That this form of free libido might even have other women as its object—that women could be lesbian— remained in the shadow of the criminal law that normalised lust. Women who love their way into the bodies of other women, who penetrate them, plunge into them, dissolve in them, without the need for a penis, without any inclination to reproduce or any vision of permanence—the only reason that didn't seem threatening to the judges was that it didn't occur to them that it was possible.

—

At some point, Daniel lost his place in the centre of the classroom. At the start of the new school year—I seem to recall that it was our fifth year; we were up on the hill by then, in the middle-school buildings—he ended up sitting right at the front of class on the left, by the window and the teacher's desk, a place where nobody wanted to sit and where you only had one person sitting next to you rather than one on either side. He was out on a limb. He hadn't lost his good looks—he'd grown taller and thinner—but he was still peculiarly angular. It wasn't just his square shoulders; his movements were also strangely jerky. Daniel was good at sport and his body was becoming more and more athletic and masculine, but there was something awkward about his movements that was hard to put your finger on; you never saw him make a smooth, easy gesture; it was as if something in him were off balance, not quite plumb.

I was struck by that even then. But I wouldn't have known quite how to describe it at the time.

Another thing that struck me was the way Daniel played ball. It didn't matter whether it was football or basketball or handball. He played well. And yet there was this strange mixture of restrained and unrestrained energy. He was both too strong and too weak, too controlled and too uncontrolled. I once broke my wrist trying to dodge one of Daniel's throws. It wasn't his fault, of course. But it was symptomatic, all the same. We were playing dodge-ball on the stony court outside the gyms. Daniel was on the opposite team and I was one of the last left in the game. When he got the ball, I instinctively backed away; he hadn't even raised his arm, hadn't even aimed at me, and already I was shrinking back. By the time the ball came hurtling towards me I was falling, stumbling backwards, and I ended up crashing down onto my right hand. When the ball actually hit me, my wrist bone had already splintered. Daniel got at least as much of a shock as I did.

Other boys were clumsier than Daniel, more unlikable, more clownish, more uptight. Some were teased because their voices took so long to break, leaving them trapped in a kind of limbo between childhood and manhood; others were ridiculed because they were swotty or fat. But those boys were picked on only sporadically; they were on the margins anyway and were by and large left alone. With Daniel it was different. There was no real reason why he should have dropped out of the group. But suddenly there he was, out on a limb, and something had changed in his eyes. He was no longer the boy who had reacted so calmly when the others had bossed him around on that first day, no longer the boy who could make it quite clear if he didn't want something, who didn't really care what the others thought. You could see he was scared now. It was presumably this fear of being banished to the margins that had pushed him out of the centre.

Then the humiliations began. The whispering when he said something. The half-concealed laughter. The lowered gazes whenever Daniel tried to catch the eye of someone who had only recently been his friend, but now rejected him. An invisible mass pushed its way between him and the rest of the class, as if his body were suddenly padded with a layer of foam, preventing him from getting too close to the others and at the same time making him seem slower, more sluggish, more ponderous.

I felt sorry for Daniel. There was no reason why he should suddenly be so isolated; it was awful to look on and watch the others' rejection take root in him, to see him lose strength, see his searching eyes gradually grow dull and turn in on themselves. Insecurity crept into his every move; every gesture he made seemed unnatural, and like a frail old person afraid of falling, Daniel moved with increasing caution. You could see the humiliation weighing on him, breaking him down, turning him into somebody else. He became even clumsier, even quieter and—perhaps worst of all—he became needy. He sought out affection, laying bare all the vulnerability of adolescence and putting himself at the mercy of the entire class.

For a while the cruelty went on covertly, a secret language, a code known only to the students, but eventually it became visible—so much so that even our class teacher couldn't fail to notice. Daniel had things thrown at him, he was spat at, he was locked in the stinky equipment room together with a jute sack full of volleyballs; somebody left a used tampon on his desk. I don't know how long our teacher pondered the question of how she could help Daniel without explicitly broaching the topic and humiliating him even further. But one day she asked Johannes and me, the two form captains, to come and talk to her. She'd like us to protect Daniel, she told us: we should sit next to him, one on either side, to screen him from the other pupils' hostility. I don't know how she explained this move to Daniel.

It was only then that I realised Daniel had never defended himself. He hadn't reacted to any of the insults, but remained silent and raw. You can only defend yourself as the person you are attacked as, Hannah Arendt once said,[23] meaning that if you are attacked as a Jew you have to defend yourself as a Jew. But how do you defend yourself if you're attacked as a weakling, a misfit, an outsider? Especially as Daniel wasn't any of those. Wouldn't anything he said have been interpreted as the response of a weakling?

There he sat, that large, square-shouldered boy, and on either side of him, the two of us, both smaller than him.

—

Was it really on the syllabus or had Kossarinsky simply sidestepped the requirements of the education board? I don't know. But I remember how happy he looked at the start of the school year, when he came into the music room with a pile of scores and cassettes in his arms, and bounced up onto the little stage where the grand piano stood, ignoring the adolescent recalcitrance that was making itself felt in the rows before him. He still got us to sing at the beginning of every music lesson; he still listened to us with the implacable look of a connoisseur that made the less musical among us fall silent rather than disappoint him with tuneless droning. But it was a long time since Kossarinsky had been content just to teach us to listen. In a state of relentless euphoria, he had spent the past years initiating us in music as text, and now he wanted us to read the architecture of composition, to learn to decipher the structures of various musical forms.

It was easy enough at first. Or at least that's what we thought. Kossarinsky got us to sing 'Dona Nobis Pacem', signalling to us when to come in, listening out for the choristers, satisfied with what he heard. Then he asked us to describe the structure of the canon or round, a musical form so familiar to us that it had never struck us as special. He was pleased when we gave him all the terms he had been hoping to hear: the music was made up of repetitions; it began with a theme; one voice sang a melody—then the motif was taken up by the second voice, and the third and the fourth, each imitating the one before. That was what Kossarinsky had been waiting for—he had wanted one of us to come up with the word 'imitation', and already he was at the piano, striking up various motifs that echoed one another—nothing that we knew: Mozart's fugues for piano, Max Reger's Variations and Fugue on a Theme by Bach. He was giving us a taste of what awaited us in the weeks and months to come, and it was soon clear that we would be doing more than recognising simple canonical structures. Kossarinsky let the music run away with him—now he was jumping ahead, playing a few bars of Shostakovich. We had a vague feeling that he wasn't going to be satisfied with a bit of singing and listening.

He stopped playing and grew serious, collecting himself—or rather, collecting us. Then, softly and assuredly, he began to play Bach's fugue in D-sharp minor, BWV 853, from the first book of *The Well-Tempered Clavier*. After that, the work began. Kossarinsky passed around the music without a word and began by asking us to use our knowledge to puzzle out as much as we could—that the theme is presented in the first two and a half bars in the middle voice, imitated by the upper voice in the third bar and finally taken up by the lower voice in the eighth bar. He got us to sing the theme so that the sequence of notes could impress itself on our minds and we'd be able to identify it in all its permutations.

Fugue, from the Latin *fuga*, meaning 'escape', was, Kossarinsky told us, a musical form, a compositional principle where various voices 'chase' after a theme. Although strictly speaking a fugue is made up of not just one theme (the subject) but also a second theme (the countersubject), Kossarinsky had chosen to teach us about the form using the D-sharp-minor fugue—a fugue that has no countersubjects, but thirty-five entries, each offering a different permutation of the main idea.

Over the years, Kossarinsky had taught us enough about harmony to allow us to identify the theme's motivic design—the two fifths framing a phrase made up of second intervals—and to work out the tonic and the dominant seventh. But that wasn't all.[24]

He wanted to explain the grammar of fugue to us, to acquaint us with the principle of subject and countersubject, the processes of development, inversion, augmentation and rhythmic variation. He wanted us to be able to interpret the metric and harmonic aspects of a fugue. In all my years of music lessons with Kossarinsky, nothing was as important to him as this. He had introduced us to polyphony, we had studied sonatas and symphonies and later even learnt how to read and notate the *basso continuo* (which certainly wasn't on the syllabus—a biographical note on Beethoven's outstanding skills as a *continuo* player had provoked some innocent question, and before we knew it, Kossarinsky had added *basso continuo* to the program). But nothing seemed to him more relevant to life than the structure of fugue in *The Well-Tempered Clavier*. For Kossarinsky, the architecture of music was more than just the architecture of music; it was a language whose syntax would shape the way we thought. He didn't explicitly teach us about structures setting normative limits while simultaneously providing scope for free play, but it was there in the music that he helped us to understand.

Our bodies set the rhythm at that time. We were growing too quickly or too slowly; every day something in us seemed to shift or swell or change. We watched bloody and milky fluids emerge from us at appropriate or inappropriate times—blood and vaginal juices, and sperm and sweat. We eyed ourselves suspiciously, as if we were strangers, at the same time longing for those signs of alienation; we were at once alarmed and relieved when our first pubic hair appeared—alarmed because it seemed to disfigure our nudity, and relieved because it meant that our sexuality, for so long a more or less invisible source of preoccupation to us, was now pushing its way into the open at last. We matured from 'half ripe' to 'ripe' and experimented with masturbation. I masturbated alone, and suppose the other girls did too, but the boys went in for group wanking contests as if it were the Federal Youth Games, presumably without suspecting for a second that they were doing something that could actually give pleasure—or indeed have homoerotic overtones.

We were angry or despairing, tired or lustful; we certainly weren't 'well-tempered', from the Latin *temperare*, meaning 'to blend properly or order'. Nothing about us was ordered or properly blended, and worse, we were plagued by insecurity, because we felt out of joint with the world; nothing was in its place, least of all us; everything seemed incongruous—too embarrassing, too daunting. We were growing into something without knowing exactly what—and in my case without knowing whether I even wanted to.

I wanted to discover desire and enjoy it, but on my own terms. Sexualised but only 'half ripe', that's what I wanted to be, because I had no desire to be 'manable', if it meant submitting to somebody else's lust. I wanted to stay half ripe, so that my own lust could continue to develop and wouldn't atrophy—so that there would always be another variation, another voice, another permutation of the original theme.

There we were, learning a musical language, analysing the world of fugue, a world concerned with questions of model and imitation, norm and difference, the appropriation of a theme—all the things that were silently gnawing at me. Glenn Gould may have complained that the fugue 'is not a form as such, in the sense that the sonata (or, at any rate, the first movement of a classical sonata) is a form', but to me that seemed its great benefit, making it a model for the way I saw desire—not a form, 'but rather an invitation to invent a form'.[25]

—

Leonce: Dance, Rosetta, dance, so that time can follow the beat of your pretty feet.
Rosetta: My feet would rather go out of time.[26]

Defining what is yours begins with a *no*.

It begins with a refusal, with the sense that you want something other than what is expected. This unease at what is asked of you may be hazy—no more than a funny feeling. You won't necessarily have an alternative in mind; it's enough to know what is out of the question for you. With this first *no* you begin to define what is yours. At this moment, when something seems less self-evident than before, when a certainty is suddenly uncertain, the unquestionable suddenly doubtful—at this moment, in this crack, the self emerges.

This isn't the same as situating the self in defeat or failure. Discourse on lesbians has established the notion that lesbian desire is an absence of desire, as if homosexual women lacked something, as if their sexuality were in some way defective. Perhaps some people find the notion more palatable than the idea that lesbian desire is a specific form of desire—that if lesbians reject a certain thing, it's because there's something else they find more beautiful, more profound, more exciting. Homosexual women desire women because they do desire, not because they don't.

That *no*, that crack, is only the beginning.

There were certain guidelines I didn't want to keep to, certain rituals I didn't want to join in. I may not have known what I wanted or why, but I knew what I didn't want, what I couldn't bring myself to do; I knew when I was on my own, rejecting something everyone else seemed to find normal. Maybe I was lucky in this intuitive refusal; maybe it protected me from experiences that would have made me feel out of place. I pulled out, stayed down, didn't budge, like jetsam left by the tide. The *no* wasn't even much of an effort. I don't know exactly when it started, but I remember the first time I felt real astonishment at the others for wanting something that only disgusted me—binge drinking.

I didn't like alcohol. Beer and chasers, vodka and gin may, like marijuana, have been markers of coolness, but besides disliking the taste of all these drinks, I was horrified at the effect they had on the others. My friends seemed to disappear. Once drunk, they became warped, alienated from themselves, and if there was one thing I wanted in those teenage years, it was to be my own person, to strip myself of anything alien to me, fend off anything potentially warping. Growing up couldn't mean turning out like the other grown-ups; it meant growing out of oneself, unfurling—not pulling an outside on over the inside, but turning the inside out.

Alcohol ratcheted up the atmosphere of those late-night gatherings. Hardly a party where I didn't end up mopping vomit in the early hours of the morning, grateful that I had something to occupy me and wasn't just hanging around gormlessly while my plastered schoolmates from 'good' middle-class families tried to wedge their hosts' dachshund into a Chinese vase or dismantle one of those wood-panelled bars popular in basement party rooms at the time. Hardly a night where one of the boys didn't slash open the palm of his hand, trying to karate chop the top off a bottle of beer; hardly a night where the guests didn't drink themselves to oblivion and then throw themselves at each other, all inhibitions shed.

I remember standing, leaning against a wall on one of those drunk and disorderly evenings, watching my friends change beyond recognition, watching girls I'd known for years act in ways that were incomprehensible to me, suddenly self-conscious in the presence of boys they'd known for just as long, suddenly coy. I was no less eager to be liked, of course, and no less concerned that the right boy should like me—it wasn't the anxious hankering that disturbed me; it was the intellectual self-mutilation that seemed to come with my friends' insecurity. An unquestioning submission had taken over these girls' gestures, leaving confident, intelligent beings strangely altered.

It made no sense to me. Something split and I didn't want to be a part of it, couldn't accept the others' impassive acceptance of their new roles. I watched them as if they were characters in a play, the other side of a curtain, and I just couldn't imagine myself acting in that play—the costumes didn't fit; the characters and their lines were alien to me.

Daniel often stood next to me towards the end of those increasingly out-of-hand parties; it was always possible that the boys wouldn't stop at the dachshund and the nouveau-riche furniture, but might also vent their aggression on him. He'd come and stand next to me the way you stand under a tree in the rain, and we'd watch the girls disappear into the bedrooms, tottering and submissive. There were couples piled up on the living-room armchairs and sofas too, while others stood at the bar mixing themselves revolting concoctions. Daniel was used to drinking; he drank a lot with the nursery gardeners—beer and chasers at knock-off time, when the trees had been planted and the heavy tools put away.

We'd stand together in silence, watching the others. Perhaps that would have been the moment to talk about what we had in common, what set us apart. Perhaps everything would have turned out differently if we had. Together we might have found a language to explain what was stopping us from cavorting with our friends—a word for our sense of unease at what seemed to come so naturally to the others.

Why didn't I just ask? Why didn't I just say what disturbed me? Why didn't I tell Daniel how glad I was to have him there next to me—not to have to be on my own? With two of us it would have been so much easier to find out what we felt, what was keeping us on the margins of the scene before us. Maybe Daniel was bothered less by the alcohol and more by the escalating violence. Maybe he already knew that he didn't desire girls; maybe he was simply afraid of being rejected; maybe he thought he no longer belonged. Maybe.

I missed the moment.

—

Lying has become a life companion. I have written that sentence and deleted it again three times. I wish it weren't true and so, lying, I overwrite it once more, but it remains true. Lying accompanies me wherever I go, offering itself, insinuating itself, always at the ready, a threat to truth. There are circles of truths—different degrees of truth that form around the innermost circle that is my lust— my living, changing, deepening desire. And what I say about it.

Closest to the centre there is silence, thrusting its way before truth like a shield, hemming it in. Then there are rings of extended and abbreviated truths; there are gaps, unwritten surfaces, stories that get left out or altered— sometimes only in part, sometimes altogether—and last of all, in the outermost ring, there is the plain, unvarnished lie.

I don't suppose that's anything special. Most people live in similar circles of silence and speech, although it isn't always desire that's at the centre. Some things are kept silent through forgetfulness, because they're not important or significant enough; others are kept silent through guilt or fear. Sometimes taboo zones are handed down through the generations, governing day-to-day life without ever being questioned. People hush up their own shame, or that of others. They deny strengths or weaknesses. Sometimes an illegitimate child is hushed up, or a disability; sometimes a person's happiness, a particular talent, a gift that is out of place in the world it has sprung up in, a sensitivity at odds with a harsh milieu—anything that is considered too complex, too hard to explain, too intractable for an ordinary conversation among strangers—all that can end up being trivialised, romanticised, normalised.

It's usually banal questions that propel me from the innermost circle of truth into the next, where I start to hold myself back, leave things out, conceal things.

'Are you married?'

That's the classic. It's something I'm often asked on my travels—in Haiti and Albania, Iran and Gaza, places where people who love the way I love can be humiliated and raped, indicted and executed. 'Are you married?' The question usually surfaces in the course of a long discussion, and often there is a large audience. A short-haired woman asking questions, a foreigner—it's like an exotic spice; everyone wants a taste. It's more informative than the telly—a chance to talk back to the western world at last, a rare opportunity to engage it in dialogue.

'Are you married?'

It's a gesture of goodwill, like a glass of sweet tea—an offer, an opening, something to inspire trust. Because for the people I talk to in Jenin or Port au Prince, *we're all married*. For them, the question is a kind of safeguard, like a piton driven into a rock face by a mountaineer—something stable that allows you to keep climbing, something you can come back to, should it prove less safe higher up.

'Are you married?'

Of course she'll say yes, they think—after all, who isn't married? Even women who travel the world are married—even women with a job that takes them far from a household they should really be taking care of. All right, so presumably their husbands have rather different ideas about marriage than people have here, but they're married all the same—*we're all married*…And from marriage the conversation can move on to children and family—all that creates trust.

All conversations among strangers should start with the similarities; that way, the differences that are bound to crop up sooner or later will be more bearable, won't open such gaping abysses.

What can I say? I know nobody's expecting a nuanced answer. The truth is, I'm *not* married. That's a relatively straightforward answer; it isn't even a lie. But do I say it? If I reply: 'I'm not married', it's nothing but the truth, but it brings a whole trail of misassumptions in its wake, some of them spectacularly funny.

Not long ago, a union leader in Rafah, in the southern Gaza Strip, offered to make me his third wife.

His intentions were gallant; it seemed to him a more than generous offer to a woman who was clearly over eighteen and still unmarried. He made a point of stressing that it was one of the advantages of Islam that you could be married to several women at once. Much to my interpreter's horror, I got her to ask whether that also applied to me. This caused general hilarity—not because the striking truck drivers seated around the union leader had any idea I might have meant it literally (could I too have several wives under Islam?), but because the notion of reverse polygamy, that a *woman* might have three *husbands*, was so ridiculous to them that they could only laugh.

On that occasion things went relatively well, but the discussions don't always take such a fortunate turn. Saying that I'm not married can provoke reactions of pity and dismay.

'So you're alone?'

What next? Do I say: 'No, I'm not alone'? And then what? If I leave it at that, everyone can breathe a sigh of relief. 'Oh good, she's not alone,' they think, and silently conjure a man at my side, only wondering uneasily how a woman can have a boyfriend and not get married. It doesn't even occur to anyone that I might have a girlfriend.

The Russian-American poet Joseph Brodsky once wrote about his reluctance to own up as a child to being Jewish. 'The real history of consciousness starts with one's first lie,' he says,[27] and describes having to fill out a form in his school library in Russia that asked for his 'nation-ality': 'I was seven years old and knew very well that I was a Jew, but I told the attendant that I didn't know.' The remarkable thing about this episode is Brodsky's expla-nation for his lie: 'I wasn't ashamed of being a Jew, nor was I scared of admitting it. [...] I was ashamed of the word "Jew" itself—in Russian, "yevrei"—regardless of its connotations.' What disturbed the boy, the adult writer tells us, was not the fact of his belonging to Judaism. He wasn't ashamed of his religion or his origins; he was ashamed of the singularity of the word: 'When one is seven one's vocabulary proves sufficient to acknowledge this word's rarity, and it is utterly unpleasant to identify oneself with it.'[28]

In the situations I get myself into on my travels, I often feel something similar. I'm not ashamed of being unmarried or having a girlfriend; I'm not uncomfortable with my life as a homosexual woman—but I am acutely aware of the rarity of the words and concepts in the context in which I find myself. My homosexuality is always some-thing unusual, something that needs explaining, excites attention.

Ought I simply to lie, like the young Brodsky? All I'd have to do would be to invent myself a biography for such situations. It would hardly be difficult. I'd give myself an imaginary husband and think up a job for him; our chil-dren would be grown up and out of the house, or with the grandparents while I was away. I'd only have to make a conscious decision to remain resolutely in that outermost circle whenever I was abroad, talking to people who can't conceive of a life like mine. I'd only have to say: 'Yes, I'm married.' Or easier still: 'I'm married to my photographer here.' I wouldn't even have to invent a fictional husband. But I can't bring myself to do it.

If your path has taken the opposite course, starting in the outermost ring and moving gradually closer to the centre—if you've had lies forced on you, circle after circle of social taboos and conventions that have all had to be overcome, you don't want to be driven away from the centre once you've got there. If you've had to struggle to recognise the truth about your own desire—if you've had to struggle to voice your desire and not to regard it, or yourself, as something disgraceful—you will react with particular sensitivity to the convention of lying.

Heightened sensitivity to the social practice of lying is common not only among homosexuals, but among all those who have longed for something socially unaccept-able, who have had to fight for their aesthetic, existential or political freedom in the face of resistance from their family, religion or society. Anyone who has had to be invisible or inaudible, anyone who has had to veil or disguise themselves for a time, knows the almost phys-ical pleasure derived simply from being able to speak the truth about themselves, to go out on the streets without a headscarf or with a kippa, to be a woman kissing another woman or a man wearing a dress.

Asked by a West German interviewer why she went around with dyed red and green hair—didn't she know that punk was dead?—the young East German politician Angela Marquardt replied that she was just glad to be free to express herself the way she wanted aesthetically. After a life in East Germany, where all forms of difference were hunted down and eliminated, it made her intensely happy to have the chance to be individual at last.

There are many such examples. Majeda, a friend of mine from Khan Younis in the Gaza Strip, once told me about the time she was able to leave the territory and travel to Switzerland for the Locarno film festival. During her stay, she ordered a beer in a bar, something that is forbidden at home in Hamas-dominated Gaza. She told me that it had given her such pleasure to drink a beer in public without secrecy, without having to worry about eliminating all traces of her forbidden act afterwards— hiding the glass, smashing it, getting rid of the broken pieces in a plastic bag—that when the waiter brought her second beer, she asked him to leave the first glass where it was, so that she could look at it—because it made her so happy that it could be left there for all to see: an empty beer glass.

For people who haven't always been able to take sexuality or truth for granted, lying isn't something that can be taken lightly. It took time and several stages of discovery for me to work out how I desire. I don't find it hard to talk about, either in Europe or in the Middle East, but because the truth is so much rarer and so much more uncomfortable in places like the Middle East, lying refuses to come easily to me there.

To anyone living in an urban environment full of artists and intellectuals, all this fuss about lying may seem unnecessary. In New York or Berlin, the truth can be as complex as you like; it will always be easily digested, because life there is consistently (homogeneously) heterogeneous. But travel beyond the borders of your own culture and you will find yourself confronted with different time zones and different habits; you will be made acutely aware of the discrepancy between what can be said here and what can be said there.

'No, I'm not married.'

From the moment I speak those words, anything can happen. Sometimes I leave it at that and remain vague. Then the truth behind my 'I'm-not-married' is left unresolved, and I become more and more embroiled in a conversation with people who are anxious to put things right and rescue me from my wretched life as an unmarried woman.

If you don't want to lie, you can simply speak the truth. If I were the only one involved, that would be risky, but it would be the right thing to do. Risky because somebody like me who isn't accompanied by a diplomatic corps, armed troops or official delegations, travels unprotected. I would be at the mercy of homophobic anger and radical dogma.

But I'm not the only one involved. I have to ask myself whose freedom I am protecting by speaking the truth and whose freedom I am jeopardising. How will my interpreter be treated after I've left? Would men allow me to interview their wives if they knew I desired women? Would I still be allowed to attend celebrations with women in separate rooms and hotel bedrooms, as is the custom in the Middle East? How would my driver be treated in his village after driving me around day after day? No, simply blurting out the truth without taking into account the consequences to my guides and interviewees—that's not an option.

And so lying has become a life companion, offering itself to me discreetly on all these journeys.

But there are other people to whom it could make a difference whether I am open or reticent, whether I talk or keep silent—people who love the way I love, who desire slightly differently, but have no language for their desire and often no place for it in their lives. What does it mean for them if I, of all people, am silent about my desire and my life—I, a westerner who can love my way into any body that gives me pleasure and let myself be taken by anyone I want to come for? What does it mean for these people if I conform to the norms that are oppressing them?

Isn't it cowardly not to talk about my sexuality in countries whose citizens risk their lives and freedom for the same desire?

That is the reason I always go a little too far on these journeys, pushing the boundaries a little further out each time. That's why I always speak a little more of the truth than is permitted—a little more than is decent or wise— and why, in every conversation, I do everything in my power to work my way through the rings to the centre, to the truth, to me and the other people who love the way I love.

Such conversations require time. I take a dim view of confronting others with things they are unfamiliar with and then being disappointed at their reactions. Most people I meet, in Iraq or Gaza, or even in more out-of-the-way places here in the West, may well have met homosexuals, but are unaware of the fact, because none of the homosexuals has ever risked owning up to it. This is something of an advantage; not knowing any homo-sexuals, these people have no notion of a homosexual person—only a dogmatic notion of homosexuality. That is the structural weakness of all taboos: they aren't able or allowed to name precisely what they forbid, because that itself would break the taboo.

In that respect my very presence is a surprise—a real live person who speaks out about the way she loves, and has a life like any other life, who isn't locked up or hidden away, but is right here, answering questions. That is so bewildering to a lot of people that it doesn't even occur to them to spurn or attack me. And presumably, although I can only speculate, it isn't only the mere fact of my existence that disarms them, but also the frank pleasure I take in my life. This undermines the shame that is expected of homosexuals—and of everyone who seems in any way different.

It's as if contempt of homosexuality weren't possible without its counterpart, shame. In the absence of shame, many people are glad of the chance to find out about something that is usually hidden away—some even think it doesn't exist at all where they come from. There are times when these conversations make me feel like a unicorn.

They can take an unintentionally funny turn. I remember one conversation with a vet in rural Argentina. We were in a car together and he grilled me on the subject of my sexuality, starting with the practical aspects— how did you actually go about things, without a cock (heterosexual men can tend to overestimate penises and underestimate size)—and progressing to theory: why was I homosexual? It wasn't the time or place to get started on Shere Hite or general studies and statistics on female sexuality.[29]

Hadn't I ever slept with men?

'Oh yes.'

Didn't I like it?

'Oh yes.'

That threw him.

'It's just more exciting with women.'

He reflected. Something told me he wouldn't simply accept that.

'Why?'

Now it was my turn to be thrown. It's easy to shrug off the question, but it's not so easy to give a precise answer. To begin with, I told him, because I fell in love with a woman—an individual, not just a body—and her sex was irrelevant to me. And later, I said, because I kept falling in love with women and, more importantly, because I wanted to sleep with women, even when I wasn't in love with them. Because I happen to like loving my way into women's bodies, because they arouse me, because it gives me pleasure to arouse them. Was that answer enough?

Thinking about it, I realised that a better answer would probably be: because there are no rules, no traditional historical practices. Lesbian sex is more exciting than heterosexual sex because it isn't normalised by images or narratives, because categories like active, passive, male, female don't exist, because there are no guidelines telling us how to have sex or what is supposed to arouse us (or so few that they haven't managed to curb my imagination), because sexuality and even lust can be reinvented when two women have sex, because it's always surprising, because it isn't fraught with historical baggage that any woman would resist, because if any power games are initiated in the rush of desire, they are open and symmetrical, because desire comes and comes again, and finally, because lust between women is unending.

But does that explain the 'why'? Can it be explained? Do heterosexuals have an answer? Why don't *they* ever stop to ask themselves why they desire the opposite sex? How can they be so sure they'll never have homosexual desires? Why doesn't anyone ask heterosexual men whether they sometimes feel the urge to be taken? Why should the idea be so unthinkable? Why should they be so sure of the answer? Why does no one ask heterosexual women when they first noticed that they desired men? (Sometimes I'm afraid certain women might say they hadn't ever noticed.) Why should heterosexuals take their sexuality more for granted than any other?

Before I could answer properly, he said:

'Are you sure you'd never sleep with a man again?'

'No. I'd sleep with Brad Pitt right away.'

Wham. I shouldn't have said that, of course. Soon I was caught up in an absurd discussion about sex with Brad Pitt. Wouldn't he sleep with Brad Pitt, I asked—I admit that I find it hard to imagine that anyone might *not* want to sleep with him. He was horrified:

'No, of course not.'

The answer came too quickly. He hadn't really asked himself the question—or hadn't wanted to—hadn't wanted to imagine sleeping with a man or to stop and ask himself if he might be able to desire a man. He seemed to find the very idea threatening.

Is that it? Does what we want depend, among other things, on what we can imagine—what we are *able* to want? Does our desire depend on what we can fantasise? And do our fantasies depend on what we dare to fantasise? Is lying only as convenient as it is because it's the only thing that allows us to curb our imagination?

I'm not saying that every fantasy has to be everybody's cup of tea (or that everyone, male and female, would sleep with Brad Pitt...). Of course desire has its limits; of course it can expand and contract, but I think the pleasure we take in our lust is deeper when it can be questioned and challenged—when we allow our fantasies free rein before deciding to reject them. Perhaps homosexual desire gives me more scope to fantasise, creates more space for an undefined lust where more is possible.

I like talking to people who find my desire incomprehensible, because even to me it's by no means self-evident. Such conversations give me a reason to return to my desire and try to understand it myself; they make me look at it as something that really is incomprehensible—and each time I examine it in this way, it only seems to grow deeper.

—

Loneliness is a feeling I associate with the sound of cobblestones. Even today a numb grief invades me when I find myself driving over old cobbles in some part or other of the world and hear that rhythmic clatter. I know why. I can place it. I know when and where the sound first surfaced and the grim association was formed.

I was sitting in the back of the car. The houses on the harbour road rolled past on the right; on the left, big-bellied ships were being repaired in the brightly lit docks. Up ahead at the end of the road, level with the old fish market, the road made a sharp bend to the right, a spot I loved because you had to pick up speed as you took the curve, so as to make it up the hill. Tucked in the corner, a blue illuminated sign gleamed over the door of the bar called 'Fuck'.

Markus and Sven were talking quietly in the front. We'd been dancing together in a club in the centre of town and were on our way home. Neither Markus nor the slightly older Sven was my boyfriend, but the three of us liked going out together, talking or dancing, as intimate as a litter of pups. That's what I thought, anyway. I liked them both. I liked the silence after the loud disco and the slow drive through the night.

But this time there was no bend. This time the car didn't pick up speed. I glimpsed the 'Fuck' out of the corner of my eye and the next thing I knew we were taking a left, leaving the tarmac road and heading west.

This was where the jolting began. The road narrowed and then forked; there was a scraggy strip of green running down the middle and on either side stood the low-slung fishmongers' warehouses. I knew the area only by day.

I'd often been here to buy fresh fish with my mother, usually for special occasions. I particularly liked it when she stopped the car right in front of the warehouses, which had entrances half a storey up to make it easier for the suppliers to load the icy boxes of fish and seafood into their trucks. I liked the functional look of the place and the no-frills shopping—no display cases, no trolleys, no proper salespeople—just fresh fish, wrapped in newspaper and put in a plastic bag or, if you bought a lot, in polystyrene boxes.

But where the vans usually parked, there were now prostitutes, standing in the half darkness. Sven slowed the car, not just to get a better look, but because all the cars driving through the red-light district by the harbour at this hour were moving at a crawl. Slowly the beam of our headlamps came closer to the women, and one after another they stepped out, cajoling, feigning invincibility—old whores and young whores, cool or insistent, desperate or indifferent, women whose years of night work showed, women conscious of their beauty, flaunting their superiority over the more down-at-heel and the punters.

Streetwalkers in town were as ordinary as pilots on the river, showmen at the fair or brokers at the stock exchange. I was used to seeing them. I was also used to the disparaging looks they directed at me, a young woman encroaching on their patch who might spoil their business. They weren't just part of the scenery here in the red-light district—no mere bittersweet erotic folklore; they were also part of the social reality of this supposedly cosmopolitan city. Businessmen proud of the town's unpuritanical attitude to sex took their Japanese and American clients to the classy Café Cherie—or the rather less classy Salambo, where they'd be pulled on stage for a live fuck—but at the same time they despised the seediness and brutality of the prostitutes' irregular lives, and would always use the old-fashioned euphemism 'girls' homes', rather than let the word 'brothel' pass their lips.[30]

Moralising about prostitution was a thing of the past. Moralising about prostitutes wasn't. 'Slut' and 'tart' were common insults; women who sold their bodies for money were still regarded as 'lost' or 'fallen', though purchasing the sexual services of these 'sluts' was common practice and certainly didn't leave the male clients lost; they were free agents. It was considered enlightened and emancipated to have a relaxed attitude to sex as a service; people thought it was time sex was freed from repressive notions of morality and bourgeois family values, time it was separated from the discourse of love and monogamy—all that seemed liberating, even if it was impossible to reconcile with the bleak images of the women I saw at the side of the road as we drove past.

It's incredible how long this ideology has survived—how long people have gone on playing down the social conditions of prostitution and tolerating exploitation. It's still hard to broach the topic without being accused of being uptight, sententious or bourgeois. People still don't like talking about human trafficking as a global economic business.[31] A fear of seeming illiberal continues to resonate; the convention of extolling prostitution as an emancipatory achievement persists.

Back then, I'd never seen the red-light district as a reason for moral outrage. There was sex on offer. All over. In all shapes and sizes. So what?

But this was different. The women were right next to the car window; I could see them up close—their breasts, bulging out of their low-cut tops, their flowing hair, their provocative bodies, right against the passenger door where Markus was sitting, half turned-on, half embarrassed. Sven was the same. Having got themselves into this situation, they were both somewhat out of their depth.

I listened to their breathless remarks, heard how horny the thought of power was making them—the whores' promise that those bodies were all theirs for a few notes. It didn't bother the boys that the money would end up in the hands of the lanky, permed pimps who were loitering nearby—or go straight to the dealers.

Nor did it bother them that I was sitting in the back

of the car. I have seldom felt as lonely as I felt at that moment, jolting over the cobblestones of the red-light district as my two friends pondered which of the long line-up of women they liked best, which would fulfil their sexual fantasies, which would know how to do things they hadn't even begun to fantasise about. They laughed and bragged, lecherous and inexperienced and so insatiable that when we reached the end of the road—just as I was about to heave a sigh of relief that the awful spectacle had come to an end, just as I was thinking we were going to take the road up the hill at last—Sven turned the car, spinning it once around the green strip in the middle, and drove back to the start of the red-light district.

I felt like dying.

I had no place there. I was extraneous. The boys had forgotten all about me. Or perhaps it simply hadn't occurred to them that there were differences between us—a difference in sex, but also a difference in desire. They didn't stop to wonder what the girl on the backseat made of it all.

Sitting there, I found myself trapped in a double identity. I sympathised with the prostitutes. In the sexual duality of the world, I saw myself reflected in them. I was like them. I too could be looked at like that, with that same blind gaze that saw without seeing; the same words could name my breasts and bum and legs, as if they were detachable doll parts. In the end, it wasn't impossible that

I could be deprived of my subjectivity like them, the agents of male lust—even in the non-passive role, their feigned dominance was nothing but an instrument of exchange.

Another reason I identified with the prostitutes was that I chose to—because they were outsiders, because other people looked down on them, because although they provided their services to men in the city centre, their lives were lived on the margins—and because, given the choice, I preferred to side with them than have anything to do with the men who bought them.

At the same time, though, I was aware of the women looking at me. And it was clear that, as far as they were concerned, I was in with the men. Sitting in the car, I was part of a clique of teenagers, separated from the women by the body of the car and by the functional procedure of kerb crawling. It was from the cars that the men looked at the prostitutes; it was from the cars that they negotiated a price—and it was on the seats of the cars that the prearranged sex took place—that the women wanked and blew and fucked at the going rate.

The women looked at the cars and at the potential clients inside; the boys eyed up the prostitutes at their window. I was the only one who didn't know where to look. I couldn't look at the women the same way the boys did. Looking at the women as objects of desire didn't work for me—and not just because I didn't yet know how to desire women. Even now, when women arouse me, I still can't look at sex workers like that.

It isn't only political and moral reasons that stop me; I'm just not turned on by it. It doesn't turn me on to look at the women, to objectify them, to know that they don't need courting—that it's irrelevant to them whether they like the look of my body, whether they're aroused by me, whether they want to find out how I smell or taste. I'm not turned on by women whose lust is measured in time and bound by emotional, sexual and financial limits, women who are easily obtainable, who can be had for money. Women I can't seduce or win over but can only buy don't arouse me—especially as I know they aren't going to let themselves be aroused by me, so that any lust and satisfaction will be necessarily one-sided. That bores me, it's alien to me, and worse than that—I would feel alien to myself in such a situation.

There I was, a woman looking at her friends looking at other women. In their gaze I saw myself as an object, and at the same time I looked at the women myself. I looked at the other women and imagined myself in their place and I looked at myself through the eyes of the boys next to me. What would their gaze do to me? What would the experience do to my friends?

The thought unnerved me. What if the boys my age came here regularly? What if they'd already done all the things I was still hoping to try out? What if their sexuality had been shaped by sex with sex workers? How arousing

143

would they find unpaid sex then? How arousing would they find me? I'd never thought about it before, presuming that the boys I knew would discover sex together with us girls. I suddenly realised how naïve I'd been. My belief that our unspoken lack of experience was something we were all in together had been a delusion—and at this moment it shattered.

I tried to make Sven and Markus's gaze my own, asking myself how I'd feel if I could look at the women as if they were strutting their stuff for me, trying to win me over as a client—how I'd feel if I knew I could take them, if I knew they'd get in the car with me to give me a blow job or let me fuck them.

But it was useless. Confused by so many ways of looking and points of view, I felt myself slip and vanish, unable to recognise myself or my desire in either of the two positions.

I don't know how long we drove around down there. But I know that the noise of the cobbles was still reverberating in my head long after we'd hit the tarmac and driven home.

—

Daniel was now completely on his own. The ostracism in the classroom hadn't let up; the hostility towards him that had begun so suddenly and unaccountably was firmly established. Now, though, the sadistic pleasure in humiliating him had given way to indifference. He had become invisible. New groups and circles sprang up from time to time, but Daniel never managed to find a place in them. He was excluded from even the most casual social interaction, never able to join in—not in the smokers' corner by the bike stands at the back of the sixth-form block, not at school-band concerts in the hall, not even at sport, where his physique and fitness ought to have made him particularly popular. He was 'out', like an untouchable, as if everyone were afraid of being infected—although no one could have put a name to his disease.

Johannes and I still sat either side of him. The direct attacks had eased off, but our class teacher thought it safer to leave us where we were. We kept an eye on him. It was hardly strange, then, that Daniel should approach Johannes and me one day and invite us to his birthday party. Still, we were completely taken aback. We had nothing against Daniel; we felt sorry for him. But we weren't his friends. We'd been parked next to him to protect him—that was all. How could he fail to understand that? Did he really think we were his friends? We never saw each other out of school or arranged to meet up. And now here he was inviting us to his birthday party.

It was a few days before we realised he hadn't invited anyone else. How could he? He didn't have anyone else. Everyone avoided him. Who could he have invited? It suggested a certain degree of realism and self-respect on

Daniel's part that he made no attempt to win over his bullies. He told us his plans for the evening: he'd like to take us to the cinema and then have dinner afterwards. At his place, next to the nursery. Just the three of us.

We knew the house. We'd been to wonderful birthday parties there—in the past, when everyone still liked Daniel. It seemed unimaginably long ago. A social eternity. Maybe he wanted to have us there because it was so long since he'd had anyone round. It wasn't something we'd thought about; we hadn't asked ourselves what it must be like to lose all your friends. Maybe he wanted to have us there because his mother was keen on the idea, keen to share in her son's life and spoil us all on his birthday.

It's only today that I begin to wonder all this, only now that everything's over. When it was too late—when Daniel was dead and I heard that he'd taken his life—this birthday party and our reaction to Daniel's invitation were the first things I thought of, the first things that came back to me, and I felt ashamed, horrified at myself.

At the time, though, we just didn't want to go to Daniel's house. That may have been mean, it may have been unfair—we both knew Daniel couldn't help his loneliness—but we just couldn't face going there. We talked it over, Johannes and I. We confessed to each other that we were both dreading the evening. We had the feeling we were being forced into an intimacy that came close to deception, because it wasn't real.

We weren't friends with him, after all. We were only there for him because nobody else was. We hadn't been picked because we particularly liked him, but because we didn't find him abhorrent—because none of the others would have dared cross us, because our teacher had decided we had a calming influence. We were glad to oblige. It was only fair; that was what form captains were for. All the same, though, it felt wrong that we were suddenly expected to feel more than we did. There was a difference between being friendly to someone and being friends with him. There was also a difference between feeling sorry for someone and liking him. We felt a little as if our goodwill were being exploited. We were prepared to protect Daniel against cruel hostility—it was our duty. But we had to be able to decide for ourselves who we were friends with outside school—you had to *want* to be friends with somebody.

We told Daniel that we'd be happy to go to the cinema with him, but that we didn't want to go back to his house afterwards. We had these awful images of the three of us sitting there all alone. It seemed too intimate. We imagined his mother's warm greetings and our own embarrassment.

I don't know whether our turning down Daniel's invitation hurt his feelings more than anything the other pupils had inflicted on him over the course of the previous years. He bore it, like everything else, with the sad composure of one who knows he's fighting a losing battle. We ended up watching a James Bond film. It went right over my head because I'd never seen a Bond film before and didn't understand the genre—and because I spent the entire film thinking about how horribly false and desperate the situation was.

Afterwards Daniel took us to the gloomy pizzeria opposite the station. I still remember exactly where we sat; we had a small table next to the door, looking out onto the main road, and the traffic lights at the crossroads shone in on us, submitting our dinner to a three-part rhythm as they changed colour. We sat there, three teenagers, Daniel, Johannes and I, and we talked about James Bond because it seemed easier than talking about what was going on in our heads. Daniel seemed pleased; you could see it in his face, in his entire body. The old strength had suddenly returned to him; he could look us in the eyes again. He enjoyed the evening with Johannes and me—and yet he was still slightly on his guard, as if he had mentally drawn in his shoulders for fear of being disappointed by us—the only ones who at least came close to being something like friends. He was slightly ashamed, too, because he knew that strictly speaking we weren't proper friends at all.

Johannes and I for our part were ashamed because although this boy deserved all our affection, although we felt sorry for him, although he was so desperately in need of friends, we didn't want to be friends with him. All that connected us, in the end, was the others' cruelty.

At the end of the evening we stood outside the pizzeria and said goodbye—Johannes and I glad it was over; Daniel glad it had happened. We were so relieved that we felt, for the first time, a sense of genuine intimacy, and we stayed on the pavement, laughing and talking, free of all sadness. We stood outside for longer than we had sat inside—a bright moment, quite distinct from everything else Daniel had been through, as if the story of his ostracism had never existed—a gift to us all. Then we got on our bikes and rode home. It was the last time I saw Daniel laugh.

—

The most beautiful moments of my childhood were all in some way related to music. Past a certain age, it wasn't just in school that I lived those moments, under Kossarinsky's strict but ebullient instruction, but also live, in concerts. I devoured everything. When the ushers closed the doors and the lights went down, when the buzz of the orchestra tuning up gradually faded, I was happier than at any other time.

As far as my mother was concerned, there was no such thing as music that was unsuitable for children. She let me hear everything: Mahler and Bruckner, familiar to me from school, but also Schoenberg, Nono, Henze.

I would sit next to her on the velvet seats of the concert hall or opera house, my hands clammy with excitement and delight. I didn't even complain about having to dress up for it, or sometimes having to endure the unbearably cheerful Mozart.

I heard Leonard Bernstein, Giuseppe Sinopoli, Michael Gielen, Sergiu Celibidache and Herbert von Karajan—directing their own orchestras, if I was lucky. I heard Alfred Brendel, Sviatoslav Richter, Itzhak Perlman and whoever else happened to be in town. The only thing I didn't like was opera. Two early attempts to interest me failed spectacularly. My parents took my brother and me to *Carmen* when we were still quite small and we got fits of the giggles and acted abominably, because we knew silly words to all the hits and couldn't get over the fact that smartly dressed grown-ups could want to listen to such hilarious songs without batting an eyelid. Later there was a second attempt, with *Turandot*. But that didn't work either.

Curiously enough, what bothered me most was the campness—the kitsch, the over-the-top gestures and, worse still, the over-the-top emotions. Everything was too loud for me, too brash, too hysterical. Maybe, too, the operas themselves were to blame; I didn't much like Bizet or Puccini and still don't. I was also disturbed by the way people burst into song with such emotion for no apparent reason, rather than just speak a straight sentence. The first opera I liked, many years later, was Benjamin Britten's *Peter Grimes*. Even today I prefer to listen to oratorios or concert versions of operas where the focus on the music is particularly intense.

Kossarinsky had now moved on to jazz, presumably because it was on the syllabus, but maybe also to make the subject more attractive to pupils having to choose between music and art for the first time. Kossarinsky brought the same passion to teaching jazz that he brought to everything, but it wasn't until we started on twelve-tone music and Schoenberg that he was in his element again. By then, though, I was going to jazz concerts, Kossarinsky's lessons always in my ears. In the Fabrik I heard Sonny Rollins, Dave Brubeck, Egberto Gismonti—and, after my school leaving exams, Chet Baker in one of his last concerts, singing and playing as softly as if he were already saying goodbye.

Through John Neumeier's ballets I got to know the music of Stravinsky, György Ligeti and Alfred Schnittke. It all began with a performance of Prokofiev's *Romeo and Juliet* with Kevin Haigen and, I seem to recall, Marianne Kruse in the main parts. Neumeier and his company opened up a new world to me. In the dancers' gestures and images, stories and bodies, I discovered things that had eluded me in literature and cinema—things that didn't feature in fiction and certainly weren't to be found in real life.

I saw Shakespeare danced before I read him. *As You Like It, The Taming of the Shrew, Othello, A Midsummer Night's Dream*—I saw all the plays in the State Opera House, and Shakespeare's gamut of emotional confusions revealed to me a plethora of feelings and relationships that didn't exist anywhere else: women were men who loved men; women carried and held and made love to women's bodies; identities shifted; gender became irrelevant; lust changed with each new object of desire—and in the wordlessness of the danced music, passions like jealousy and resentment and affection stood out so much more clearly.

My notion of love as something beyond our control comes from *A Midsummer Night's Dream*, where whoever falls under the spell of the love potion is stupefied, overcome, made to love unconditionally—blindly, even—no matter who he or she sets eyes on, no matter how unsuitable. And it's true, what Shakespeare tells us—that as long as the love philtre retains its potency, we don't notice our loved ones' long ears or furry coats; we aren't bothered by their stubbornness. We love because it happens, because it takes hold of us, depriving us of all willpower, leaving us with nothing but desire. What in Shakespeare is a magic potion can be a look, a word, a faint drawl, a slight accent, the way someone holds her head on one side, the gentle way someone strokes a dog—and whatever it is that sparks our love, it lasts as long as the philtre has effect, making everything else unimportant, superfluous, invisible. I still believe that, just as I believe that the potion can suddenly wear off, leaving the other person looking suspiciously like an ass with big ears.

The generation of soloists I grew up with, the generation that initiated me into this world, included Ivan Liška, François Klaus, Kevin Haigen, Gamal Gouda, Colleen Scott, Chantal Lefèvre and Marianne Kruse. After a time I could guess which dancer Neumeier would cast in which role: Kevin Haigen always seemed to dance the youthful, easygoing characters, prone to get confused and make mistakes, but high-spirited and boisterous. François Klaus, with his slightly larger body, danced the staider roles—Peter in the *St Matthew Passion*, for example, whose body folded in half every time it came to 'And he went out and wept bitterly'. Then there was Ivan Liška, who always gave the impression of being unapproachable—elegant but unapproachable.

Over time, I discovered my own preferences as well as Neumeier's. I particularly liked Ronald Darden, a big African-American dancer, whose aura of gentle calm put everything in the shade. He had only to come on stage to make you hold your breath; everything went still when he danced. All agitation, all inner restlessness, melted away when his gentle intensity filled the house.

Today, when I'm travelling in crisis zones and find myself in unpleasant situations—when I have to be sure that others aren't going to perceive me as alien or threatening, I sometimes imagine myself into Ronald Darden's body. I look for that same slowness inside myself, those outstretched arms that enveloped and absorbed and protected, that deep sense of assurance, and I hope I am radiating the same infectious, reconciling calm.

The real hero of my youth, though, was Max Midinet. He was more delicately built than the others, almost girl-like—half ripe rather than ripe; you wondered where in that body he drew his strength. He didn't quite fit the male roles that involved lifting or carrying female dancers. There was something different about Midinet; he always stood a little to one side, immersed in himself, though never unfocused, detached from what was going on, as if he were on another time scale.

He played Iago in *Othello*, Christ in the *St Matthew Passion* and Merlin in *The Saga of King Arthur*. For me he was always the narrator (although he wasn't the evangelist in the *St Matthew Passion*—where, incidentally, the wonderful Ronald Darden, with his beautifully aligned body, carried the cross). Midinet was always left over; he filled the gaps in the narrative without ever really belonging. I picked him out of every picture, every scene, as if he were the Archimedean point of each plot, as if his character were the key to understanding the stories.

The slender and subtle Midinet danced as if he were dancing the chorus of a Greek drama, except that he was

154

quieter and less moralising, more like an evangelist or a prophet—someone who could speak and interpret even when he was dancing.

Oddly enough, I also liked Midinet because there was a certain air of fragility about him. He wasn't really fragile, of course. He was a formidable dancer. But you were always aware of his physicality. He didn't have the suave elegance of Ivan Liška, or the boisterousness of Gamal Gouda; his dancing was effortless and yet a hint of vulnerability showed through, the pain of something unnameable and yet undeniably *there*. He was surrounded by an aura of exile; it was present in every gesture, every step, every spin.

Years after I'd left school, when I was living in another town and Max Midinet had stopped dancing, I saw him again. He had a small antiques shop just behind the opera house. I went up the few steps to the glass door and walked in—and all at once he was there before me, the dancer I had admired evening after evening, whose confident fragility I had so loved. He was still slight and lean and had the same dark curls. I didn't say anything. I thought it might make him feel as if he were on display, like his antiques, if I told him what he'd meant to me— that his way of dancing and the characters he danced had opened up new spaces to me, shown me that it's possible to live in the 'in-between', that even characters who don't quite fit in are necessary, that they have their own parts to play. All that had shaken the social order as I knew it, broken open a space for me to grow into.

With his slender appearance, his fragile yet athletic physicality that seemed to elude all male and female role assignment, Max Midinet shattered the clearly demarcated zones of the heterosexual world, where men and women were supposed to live and love.

Not long after, I read that Max Midinet had died.

—

When I was sixteen, a scandal erupted that made us realise that sexuality wasn't something private, but that it could be used, that it could act as an instrument of denunciation, and that as an epithet, whether founded or unfounded, it was capable of socially destroying people. The Kiessling Affair of 1984 revealed to us what you might find yourself up against if you were thought to be homosexual.

The social condemnation and discrimination of homosexuals was ubiquitous, but seldom visible to us. There were still youth protection units policing the toilets in public parks where gays met; there were still official records of homosexuals known as 'pink lists'. The practice of spying on gays and lesbians had been exposed in June 1980, when plain-clothes police officers took photos from a VW van after a Gay Pride march organised by the Gay and Lesbian Association and indignant demonstrators demanded the film. The plain-clothes officers refused to hand it over, and called the uniformed police.[32] It subsequently emerged that, as well as registering homosexuals in separate files, the police had equipped some men's toilets with mirror glass and surveillance rooms.

We'd heard nothing of the conflicts that were going on in the town where we lived; we had no idea that state institutions continued to take it for granted that homosexuals were treated like criminal elements, or that the gay and lesbian movement had begun to protest against such forms of discrimination. I have had to look it all up. I was living in the same town, but I knew nothing of the raids or the surveillance—and nothing of the lively activist gay scene. Perhaps I was too young. Perhaps homosexuals were marginalised to such an extent that the stories about their discrimination didn't make it into the mainstream news.

Looking through the material from the archives on homosexuality in the sixties and seventies, I have been struck not only by the number of gay activists who are now colleagues and friends of mine in Berlin, with a long history of fighting for the rights of people who desire the way I do—but also by how liberal the Liberals were in those days. A huge number of queries, complaints and petitions from members of the Free Democratic Party were concerned with the discrimination of gays and lesbians.

It took the Kiessling Affair, though, to wake us up to

what was going on. Only when a high-ranking military man was the victim of the kind of discrimination that open and less prestigious homosexuals were exposed to daily did we begin to take notice—only when Kiessling began to defend himself against the charge of homosexuality brought by the defence ministry and to protest against the treatment that followed.

What had happened?

It was a fondness for books, not for boys, that was to be Kiessling's undoing—that, and the military's fondness for rumours.[33] After the public humiliation and discharge of four-star general Günter Kiessling, it emerged that he had first aroused suspicions among his colleagues in NATO and the Bundeswehr for being a voracious reader who spent most of his time 'in a single room' of his official residence in the Belgian village of Nimy—'the book-crammed wood-panelled library'—shirking the usual pastimes of status-obsessed generals, 'such as playing golf'.[34]

Günter Kiessling's colleagues saw him as a loner— and, what's more, a devout Protestant and intellectual, who spent his free hours in academic pursuits. That made him an odd man out in the military milieu. It was enough to arouse suspicion. And it wasn't long before the suspicion developed into a rumour: Kiessling had been sighted 'holding hands' with a man. Later this allegation was elaborated on by an admiral doctor who claimed that

Kiessling had 'fiddled around with himself under his dressing gown' during his medical.[35]

In 1983, homosexuality was no longer a punishable offence in West Germany, but it still served as a vehicle of denunciation and was surrounded by political and legal ambivalence within the Bundeswehr. According to the fitness criteria of the German army, which had been brought in line with the updated version of Paragraph 175, candidates were still considered unfit for military service if their 'homosexuality [had] degenerated to a genuine perversion'. What exactly that was supposed to mean was not specified. The Bundeswehr cited their alleged duty to protect other recruits under their responsibility from the advances of homosexual soldiers.

A ruling passed by the first Military Service Senate of the Federal Administrative Court in 1979 deemed homosexuals unsuitable for the higher ranks of the army, because 'if a superior has homosexual tendencies, [there is a] danger that, perhaps without always being aware of it, he will see his subordinates not only as soldiers in his charge and under his command, but also as potential sexual partners.'[36]

Thus a mere rumour was enough to ruin General Kiessling's career in the space of a few months.

Between June and December 1983, the gossip developed first into a memorandum and then into a shabby and inadequate 'investigation' in two gay bars in Cologne (the

Tomtom and Café Wüsten), where a picture of the General was passed around—a photograph in which his uniform had been touched up. One of the men consulted thought he recognised the man in the photo as someone he'd seen ten years before; another thought it might be 'Jürgen'—'a guard in the Bundeswehr'. Before long, these statements had become watertight evidence ('he was clearly identified in Cologne's homosexual scene') and Kiessling ended up being discharged from the army.

In September 1983, minister of defence Manfred Wörner confronted Kiessling with the allegations and suggested that he report sick for twenty-eight weeks; he would be discharged with a 'Grand Tattoo' in March 1984. Kiessling denied that he was homosexual; he also denied ever having been in either of the two bars in Cologne, but after thinking it over for four days, he took Wörner up on his offer nevertheless—mainly to avoid a public scandal that might prove damaging to the image of the Bundeswehr. He assumed that more thorough investigations would in any case soon exonerate him.

But despite internal criticism of the weak evidence, the 'investigations' of the Military Counterintelligence Service only confirmed the earlier findings, and a warning was issued against Kiessling. Homosexuality was deemed a threat to the Bundeswehr ('According to Central Service Regulations 2/30 CLASSIFIED—FOUO Part C Appendix C 1 No. 3, said circumstances are a security risk'[37]), because a homosexual general was supposedly susceptible to blackmail. As Wörner saw it, an (allegedly) homosexual general had to be removed from active service and could be demeaned and discriminated against because his fear of public exposure and discrimination or even discharge was so great that he was at risk of being blackmailed by foreign intelligence services.

The Military Counterintelligence Service remarked: 'It should moreover be regarded as an aggravating circumstance that General Dr K. has so far denied his homosexual tendencies. This denial and the resulting potential for blackmail represent a significant security risk.'[38] Before others blackmail him, we'd better blackmail him ourselves. In December Wörner reneged on his previous decision and decided to discharge Kiessling earlier than originally announced, at the end of December.

The paradox of the whole episode was that, by acting as he did, Wörner himself exposed the Bundeswehr (and himself) to blackmail. Homosexual or not, it wasn't Kiessling who was susceptible to blackmail, but the minister of defence, because he was the only one who seemed to regard homosexuality as a problem. If Wörner had really wanted to protect the Bundeswehr, all he had to do was welcome Kiessling—and any other putative or genuine homosexuals—openly and publicly into the army. If they'd been accepted into the Bundeswehr *as homosexuals*, foreign intelligence services would have had no reason to blackmail them.

What defence minister Wörner hadn't reckoned with was that Kiessling would defend himself; after his discharge he even spoke out in public. He said that he wasn't homosexual, that he didn't know the bars in question and had never set foot in them. Kiessling not only defended himself against an allegation he regarded as plainly false (his putative homosexuality); he also protested against the insufficient evidence, his lack of opportunity to dispute the allegations, the poor quality of the investigations and, last but not least, the absence of grounds for his discharge—because, as he pointed out, the security interests of West Germany had not in fact been affected.

In an interview Kiessling said: 'Believe me, I'm not interested in being rehabilitated; what concerns me is that this kind of thing shouldn't happen in a state where the rule of law prevails.'[39] When the meagre 'evidence' and spurious arguments claiming that homosexuality was a security risk were at last held up to public scrutiny and debated in the Bundestag, the head of government, Helmut Kohl, called an end to the affair and reinstated Kiessling in active service in February 1984. Kiessling retired honourably later that year and was seen off with a 'Grand Tattoo'.

All that is a long time ago. But the logic of sexual denunciation and the sometimes denunciatory attempts to resist it are still with us. It is still used to force people onto the defensive; even today people think they have to defend themselves against something they could simply dismiss as false. In 2004, precisely twenty years after the Kiessling Affair, the Christian Democratic Union of Baden-Württemberg was looking for a successor for Minister-President Erwin Teufel, who had stepped down. Standing for election were Günther Oettinger and Annette Schavan. Soon rumours were circulating that the unmarried and childless Schavan was lesbian.

Annette Schavan spoke of 'slander' and a 'smear campaign'. She called the allegations 'shabby' and 'absurd'. In fact, it's shabby and absurd to act as if homosexuality were an offence or a crime—as if to 'accuse' somebody of being homosexual amounted to a smear campaign. It's mixing up categories to treat sexuality in moral terms at all.[40]

It isn't 'good' or 'bad' to be homosexual; it simply *is*, just as it isn't a moral offence to be heterosexual, transsexual or bisexual; it simply *is*. It's *one* form of loving among many—whether innate or acquired, assumed or chosen, variable or constant makes no difference because the many different kinds of desire are irrelevant to normative questions. Being homosexual doesn't make me insecure or secure, ashamed or proud; it's a fact, and that's all there is to it.

I am happy in my life in a way I could never have

imagined. I don't want to be any different or desire any differently. I take pleasure in loving the way I do—but not because it's morally better or worse than any other way.

If someone assumes I'm heterosexual, I'm not offended or pleased; it's as if someone had assumed I'm left-handed when I'm not. There are contexts in which being right-handed might have practical consequences: if you play the cello, for example, or want to buy a fountain pen—but it's not a moral category. There are contexts in which being right-handed might play a political role: if for instance retraining schemes were introduced to drill right-handed people to write with their left hands—but in such a case the social milieu would be imposing a meaning on right-handedness that right-handed people themselves had no say in.

Annette Schavan could have said: 'I'm not lesbian, but even if I were, I'd still be a better minister-president than Günther Oettinger...' She could have pointed to the Christian Democratic mayor of Hamburg, Ole von Beust, whose open homosexuality made no difference to the performance of his duties. She could have said that people who thought they could vilify anyone with rumours about sexuality in this day and age, vilified only themselves. She could have asked why it was relevant— it wasn't as if anyone seemed to care what kind of sex Günther Oettinger practised.

But in 2004, twenty years after the Kiessling Affair,

homosexuality—at least among the Christian Demo-
crats of Baden-Württemberg—was still regarded as
'defamatory'.[41]

———

It was a big wedding and I'd been looking forward to
it. The groom was a good friend of mine. Now the ceremony proper was over and those of us who had made the
journey to celebrate our friend's happiness were pouring
into a beautiful light and airy room for the reception. I
was openly gay by this time; it was no secret that I loved
women. My friends had seen and sympathised with the
shift in my desire from men to women as if I'd moved
house, from one flat to another, one area to another; they'd
shown a certain curiosity in the new neighbourhood and
how I got on there, but they hadn't made a big thing of it.

I'd gone to the wedding with my best (heterosexual)
girlfriend. We've known each other for so long, and are
so close, that to outsiders we look like a couple, a situation that my best friend, far from letting it embarrass or
upset her, seems to relish. She never makes any attempt to
clear up the misunderstanding. Once when she'd moved
in with me in Berlin for a while, a neighbour of mine,
ninety-something-year-old Frau Engel, asked her if she
lived with 'Frau Emcke'. When she said she did, Frau
Engel asked: 'And are you and Frau Emcke married?'
(Registered partnership had, I would guess, been

introduced just six months before.) 'Well,' my best friend replied, 'kind of.'

It was as a 'kind-of' married couple, then, that we entered the room where the seating plan for the wedding reception was displayed. Our hosts had gone to incredible lengths to make the occasion an enjoyable one—not just for themselves but also for their guests and friends. A lot of thought had gone into the preparations; everything had been planned down to the last detail, lovingly and tastefully, and we were looking forward to the dinner and the new people we would meet.

When we came to the table we'd been allocated, we saw that my best friend and I were sitting next to each other. We looked about us. At all the other tables where the guests were starting to take their seats, men had been put next to women; we were the only women without a man between us. Then the others at our table began to show up. For minutes I stared at them speechlessly, each in turn, not sure whether to believe what I was seeing. It was hardly credible—we were sitting at the 'gay table'.

We sat there, slightly stunned. In disbelief I asked the person opposite me whether I was right in thinking this was the queer table—there was another gay couple besides me and my 'kind-of wife', a bisexual woman and a doubtful. I think a heterosexual relative had been thrown in too; not everyone at the table was homosexual. But there were no gay wedding guests who *weren't* sitting at our table. For a while this gave us something to talk about. If the seating plans were based on sexual practices, what did that tell us about the other tables? What if they'd all been similarly organised? We looked about us and let our imaginations run riot: the six people at the next table liked anal sex; two tables further on was the role-play table; those people over there had a thing about prostitutes; the next lot were into bondage...

It was presumably 'well meant'. Presumably our hosts wanted to show how 'tolerant' they were; they'd clearly gone to some trouble. But who wants to be friends with someone who 'tolerates' her? Who wants to be friends with someone who, after years of friendship, thinks that her defining feature is her sexuality? How 'well meant' would it have been if there had been a table for black people—if the wedding guests had been predominantly white and the only black people there had all been put at the same table—if there hadn't been enough black people to go round, so our hosts had made up the numbers by throwing in a Latino and a white person or two who wouldn't mind being thought black? It would have been immediately obvious to everyone that such treatment was unacceptable.

I have rarely felt as gay as I felt that evening. The seating plan subjected us to an objectifying gaze. It was irrelevant whether or not I considered my sexuality the defining feature of my personality (I didn't), or that I

made a point of deconstructing and undermining traditional clichés and norms. It didn't matter what else I had
in common with the other people at my table (not a lot);
my perception of myself was immaterial that evening.
And the way others—even friends—perceived me was
brought home to me with painful clarity.

In 1832, in one of his *Letters from Paris*, the satirist
Ludwig Börne wrote: 'Some accuse me of being Jewish,
others forgive me for it, a third might even praise me for
it. But everyone thinks about it. You'd think they were
bewitched; they're all trapped in this Jewish circle and
can't get out.'[42] Börne had long been converted when he
wrote that.

That's how it felt. Some accuse us of desiring a certain
way, others forgive us for it, a third might even praise us
for it. But everyone thinks about it. You'd think they were
bewitched; they're all trapped in this sex circle and can't
get out.

An individual is made up of any number of qualities. I'm a philosopher and a journalist, I write about
landscapes of violence and support Borussia Dortmund.
Fried onions and anti-Semites make me feel sick. I like
bars, especially when they're dark and a bit sleazy. I like
roaming around deserted areas, preferably along railway
lines. I'm not a wine buff, but I like my tea; I always take
a tin of loose Assam with me on my travels. My world
is made up of voices, sounds and noises—and above all

music; I'm an acoustic person, but make up for it by seeing practically nothing. Overly bourgeois events bring on an irresistible urge in me to misbehave. I never fail to feel happy when I arrive in New York; my family moved away from Germany and then back again, and my life is shot through with a longing for foreign places that feel like home. I collect photographers and their pictures—the photographers as friends and the photos to hang on the walls of my flat. I love the light in Jerusalem. Any of these things would have given me more to talk about than the way I desire—although I suppose my taste in bars isn't entirely unconnected.

For a while we joked about the grotesque situation, but soon a dull anger began to rise. I had fantasies about seducing a random (heterosexual) woman in the toilets. Since, on top of everything else, our table was right at the edge of the room, conveniently close to the exit and the toilets, it wouldn't have been far to go, and in amongst all those wedding guests I was bound to find someone who was up for it. Not that I made a point of seducing guests at wedding receptions, but Hannah Arendt is right: 'You can only defend yourself as the person you are attacked as', and in my helpless rage I felt an urge to retaliate in the role I'd been given and live up to expectations.

If the only thing defining us was sex, I wanted to fuck.

We aren't only what we want to be. We are also

what others make of us. Being homosexual doesn't only mean desiring in a certain way. I am not homosexual just because women arouse me and I like waking up in their arms, because I want to be loved by a woman and touch her breasts and take her crotch in my mouth, because I like the taste of women—their skin, their smell, their voices. I'm not homosexual just because I like seducing women and taking them and being taken by them. I'm not homosexual just because I desire the way I do and love the way I do.

No. I am also homosexual because I have stories like this to tell—stories in which I am stripped of my sense of self and stamped with the badge of sexuality, stories in which I am marked out as different, stories that are probably familiar to all gay, lesbian and transgender people, stories in which we are put on show, perhaps as perverse or sick, perhaps as hypersexualised or asexual, unmanly or unfeminine, but certainly as different. We know stories of rejection and ostracism, stories of restaurateurs who refuse to serve us, of being turned away from hospitals where our loved ones are lying sick. We are familiar with laws like the Registered Partnership Act, which supposedly recognise us as equals, but in fact only enshrine inequality. We know what it is to have someone explain to us we're only allowed to adopt 'difficult' children—as if they were such hopeless cases that even perverts like us couldn't screw them up any further. We know stories in which there is no place for us—or a separate table.

I am more homosexual than I feel, because my homosexuality means more to others than it does to me. I am more homosexual than I think—and homosexual in a different way—because others have warped views of homosexuals, warped notions, fraught with the history of marginalisation. I am homosexual because there is a history of repressing and criminalising homosexuality. I am homosexual because it isn't easy to pit new views and notions against the old ones, to undermine them and give them new meaning. I'm homosexual because apparently, although it was possible in the ancient world, the practices we live can't simply be practices. I'm homosexual because a lot of people can't get it into their heads that homosexuality is only one language of desire among many, a language that feels right to me. I'm homosexual because homosexuality is a label, a historical category that takes a single practice and uses it to create an entire person, an identity, a way of life. Just as belief can't simply be part of religious practice any longer, but has had to become the overriding feature of an entire identity, a collective, I can't simply desire these days; I have to *be* homosexual. I'm a member of the gay and lesbian scene, because my 'I' is constantly being turned into a 'we' that I then accept as mine.

We should have got up and left the wedding reception; we should have taken a stand against the seating plan. That way we'd have become a real 'we', the kind that knows how to act as a collective. But we stayed put. We didn't want to pour shame on our friend or spoil the nice party. How would it have looked if we'd left? We'd have ruined our friend's day. And so we toed the line. We stayed, feeling shabby, as if we'd gone to a smart party in dirty clothes. The shame that our host should have felt clung to us—and although we'd been lumped together as a group, we felt disconnected.

Identities aren't only a matter of choice; they are also constructed, assigned, ascribed; they come accompanied by restrictions, by a history of criminalisation, by denunciation and neglect; they are bound up with prejudices, ignorance and convictions that are cited and passed on, in-jokes and conspiratorial whispers, out of sexual inhibition or contempt, handed down from generation to generation, in school books or adoption laws, films or seating plans.

I can reject that. I can find it ridiculous. I can regard my homosexuality as no more or less important than my right-handedness. But it won't make any difference to the social reality of the world where I live. I can try to sabotage things and undermine them; I can try to change reality. But until I have, it's a part of me.

What is worse, the labels that are so keen to tag and pigeonhole everything—to invent differences and mark them out—end by blurring other differences. They are too sweeping, too abstract, declaring certain qualities relevant and neglecting others. A black homosexual Harvard professor who teaches English eighteenth-century poetry has a great number of possible points of reference, affinities and similarities with others—and they are different from those of a black heterosexual window cleaner and Bulls fan in Chicago.[43]

Once we have been typecast by labels, all subtle distinctions are lost; any other features of origin or class—any social, aesthetic, political or sexual leanings are negated. All our irrational little passions and individual feelings are ironed out—any preferences or beliefs not directly related to our origins, any metaphysical intuitions not rooted in our particular religion, any unaccountable likes or interests—everything life is about is excluded.

Of course it's an achievement that Muslims—or homosexuals, or Jews—now get invited to talk shows, but so far it's tended to be in connection with the topic of radical Islam—or sex, or Israel. It's an achievement that homosexual actors are given parts in films or television series, but so far it's tended to be in the role of gay people or commitment-phobic women.[44] Turkish people and lesbians can be comedians or cabaret artists; they can make jokes about themselves and sometimes about others, not unlike court jesters, who were allowed to be critical as long as they stuck to witty verse. But to be a Turkish person and talk about tax increases, to be a cabaret artist and question the legitimacy of the war in Afghanistan, to be a lesbian actor and play sultry heterosexual mistresses—that's not quite so easy.

The myth of authenticity, so often asserted in good faith, proves to be a trap because it denies the ambiguity of seeing and reduces the diversity present in all identities to one 'genuine', 'true' form that ends up hemming us in.

What does 'authentic' mean anyway? How 'authentic' are we? Am I 'authentic'? How similar must we be? What about all the other aspects that make us the individuals that we are? Does sexuality really take precedence over everything else? Do our other defining features melt away in the face of sexuality? Isn't it a lie that class, origins, sex, religion—all the other markers of identity—play no role in distinguishing us? What about the other perspectives, the other ways of looking at shame, intimacy, social confidence and vulnerability that can make a difference to our acceptance and visibility in everyday life?

It is a curse of our time that, under the banner of authenticity and essential identity, we narrow and reduce belief, origin and desire into collective concepts. This may make sense during a political debate, but it isn't necessary afterwards. Concepts of collective identities make good rhetorical vehicles in political struggles for legal recognition, but they cannot provide a home.

—

I have forgotten when I first heard the music of Dmitri Shostakovich—perhaps on the radio, with my mother, or at a concert. I know that at some point—I can't remember the exact year—I acquired a recording of Shostakovich's Piano Concertos Nos. 1 and 2, op. 35 and 102 with Eugene List on the piano and Shostakovich's son Maxim conducting the USSR Radio Symphony Orchestra. Funnily enough, I remember the record sleeve, maybe because I loved maps even then, maybe because of the way Moscow was circled in red, as if it were the centre of the world. Although I grew up in the west, anti-Communist propaganda was by no means part of the educational repertoire of my teachers or parents, but still, it was the first time I'd seen a map with Moscow in the centre. I loved the Andante in the second concerto; I can remember listening to it and dreaming my way into the map and away. I don't know whether the recording is still available. Today I have one with Elisabeth Leonskaja on the piano.

Of course I also listened to the stuff everyone was listening to back then—Bob Dylan, Neil Young, the Velvet Underground—and like everyone else, I went to concerts—everything from Al Jarreau to Level 42— whatever happened to be in. But I didn't really think of that as music. It was more like a cocktail—social convention rather than pleasure; there was something fleeting and volatile about it. *Real* music was music you couldn't hear without emotional upheaval; it made you want to shrink to almost nothing on the outside, while on the inside you swelled with every note. That kind of music was different. I began to collect friends and fall in love with them because they were people I could listen to music with—because they loved music or introduced me to music that was different and new. Keith Jarrett and Chick Corea, the Beethoven sonatas, Olivier Messiaen, Leoš Janáček—all those I discovered with somebody else.

And then there was my love of Shostakovich—first the piano concertos, and later the Twenty-Four Preludes and Fugues, op. 87, a kind of continuation of *The Well-Tempered Clavier*. The search for motifs became a search for structures, but it still felt like a treasure hunt and there was still that additional treasure that Kossarinsky had given us along with the joy of listening: the ability to find trails and follow them.

Finally, Kossarinsky himself began to teach the music I had listened to and learnt to love on my own. Now that we were older, he had started to supplement his teaching with political and biographical details from the lives of the composers. As well as telling us about the inner logic of the composition and the historical development of the musical language, he got us to think about external factors—the cultural and social contexts and the way they had restricted or facilitated the work.

Kossarinsky told us about Shostakovich's controversial life in the Soviet Union and about the great success of his first symphony when he was only nineteen. As he talked, he sat at the grand piano in the music room, playing odd motifs from the works he was discussing. Other people make gestures to give weight to their words; Kossarinsky made music, playing almost inadvertently, as if he weren't altogether aware of it—he wouldn't play us a recording of the quartets themselves until the end of the lesson. He told us how in the West Shostakovich was regarded as a musical propagandist for the Soviet Union—an interpretation that seemed to him ill-considered and, as he put it, rather lazy. If you wanted to find out about the composer's politics, it was no good listening to the laudatory things the Communist regime said about him; you had to listen to his music—*really* listen to it.

Kossarinsky spoke and played and spoke some more, and a world opened up, more intricate and filigree and ramified than the one we knew, as if we'd reached the middle of the rhododendron, plunging through the spherical outer structure to discover the spaces and web of branches hiding within. The Soviet Union was no longer the Communist regime that featured in our social studies lessons. The East-West conflict, the Cold War, the rigid perception of the world in antagonistic terms—all that shattered to reveal what Kossarinsky wanted to make us see: one man's struggle for a (musical) language, the conflict between an individual and an ideological system, between aesthetic formalism and the prescribed norm with its demand for more traditional music.

At the end of the lesson Kossarinsky played us a recording of Shostakovich's String Quartet No. 8, op. 110 and we listened, rapt, to the opening four-note motif that begins in the cello and is then taken up canonically by the viola, the second violin and the first violin. When, in the next bars, this was followed by all the semitones in the octave, the tonal ambivalence unnerved us. I remember sitting there, physically almost unable to bear it—thrilled and bewildered and exhilarated all at once.

We had only just taken in the slow lament of the Largo when the second movement started up without warning. Kossarinsky let us listen first—to the outburst in the Allegro, the frenzy that knows only two moments of respite, in the echoes of Jewish music—then he told us about Shostakovich's criticism of Russian anti-Semitism, about his settings of texts by Yevgeny Yevtushenko in his Symphony No. 13 and the resentment it caused among Soviet officials. Everything was mixed up and everything came together; the music we had heard was unravelled and at the same time interwoven with other works of music. Little by little, Kossarinsky revealed Shostakovich's holistic approach to thinking and composing, showing us the web of quotations and references connecting the various quartets and symphonies—the echo of the first cello concerto in the theme of the quartet's third movement, and of course the D-E flat-C-B flat motif which is Shostakovich's signature,[45] his tribute to Bach, and an allusion to the other compositions he signed in the same way.

I suddenly began to think and hear music 'horizontally' as well as 'vertically'. I was fascinated by the idea that a composer could quote himself in his music, but also by his references to other contemporary aesthetic and social developments—the musical allusions, criticism and individual dissidence that were concealed but also given expression in his work.

—

He probably didn't feel anything like as brave as he seemed to me, but the first time Tom took me to the café where he was a regular—a good-looking young man, or perhaps I should say a good-looking manly boy intently eyed by the adult men at the other tables—I admired him no end. I remember climbing the steps to the entrance with him and registering the discreet nods of greeting, and as we sat down I noticed the men vying for attention in a way that went against everything I had so far considered the main feature of gay life: invisibility, secrecy, the need to remain unnoticed. Here it was the other way round. I walked into Tom's world with him, into Café Image, and realised that this was a world of its own—that homosexuality had a place and that what mattered there was looking and being looked at.

The Image was in the centre of town—not on the outskirts, not on the margins, not in the red-light district, not hidden away in some shady neighbourhood. It was in a small, elegant shopping street with fashion boutiques and a shop selling antique clocks—and the café's openness, its refusal to hide something that no one was ashamed of, made it just the place for Tom. He seemed to be the only one of us who didn't spend those years searching, whose otherness seemed to harbour neither secret nor doubt. Tom was gay—unequivocally, unquestionably and refreshingly gay.

Tom was the first man I knew to love men—the first real-life gay man to step out of the public discourse on homosexuality, like the characters in Woody Allen's *The Purple Rose of Cairo*, who step out of the film and climb down into the audience. He was the first homosexual to assume three-dimensional form in my life; he talked and laughed and swore like me; we went to the cinema together, or out dancing or swimming, and we read the same books, separated only by large tracts of the city— and by our experiences. I remained a spectator, looking on enthusiastically, but from a distance, as he climbed back into a film in which I played no part.

Tom didn't overlap with any of my schoolmates. He became a friend, although he lived on the other side of town, but more than anything he became *my* friend, changing my world without altering the social or erotic order in class or at school. Daniel never got to know Tom. Maybe it would have made all the difference to him. Maybe it would have relieved him of some of his burden, his isolation.

Tom didn't exactly make a difference to me, but he reinforced a longing in me. The world he introduced me to wasn't quite my world, even then, because I didn't desire the way he desired—but the life he wanted to live appealed to me; there was something radical about it that I found infinitely attractive because of the way it opened up new spaces.

It was as if he'd discovered a hidden wood that lay beyond the one I knew so well, a wood that despite all my explorations had escaped my notice, a wood I had no access to, because access was granted only to young men who appealed to older men—but all the same, a wood I'd have liked to explore. I had gashes in my arms and legs from jumping over barbed-wire fences and climbing into building sites; I'd roamed around abandoned houses and squats. But this was different. While the rest of us were still busy trying to leave something behind—trying to break out—Tom had already arrived.

That's not quite true. When I first met Tom, he was still living at his dad's and one thing we did have in common, apart from our passion for ballet, were the quarrels at home. No part of Tom's life was easy—I knew that, although I lived in another part of town, far from the dramas being played out in his dad's kitchen. When the arguments became unbearable, he moved out. He was the first of us to brave the adult world, going to live just north of the station in a tiny attic flat with sloping ceilings that wasn't really big enough for him unless he was sitting down. He felt out of place at school because nothing he was taught had any bearing on the life he dreamed of, and he was baffled by his schoolmates who seemed to have turned into their own grandparents before they'd even reached sexual maturity. Tom had a tendency to claustrophobia, because any form of intellectual or sexual narrowness caused him suffering.

I had also found myself by then, though in a different way. I knew with a deep inner certainty that my own guilty pleasures of voracious reading and constant, frenzied writing weren't passing fads, but would bring me lasting existential happiness—and that certainty, unlikely as it might seem in the world where I grew up, was even then part of my life, as unassailable and indestructible as Tom's certainty about his sexuality.

Unlike me, though, Tom had something light and springy about him. This was partly to do with his good looks, but only partly. Tom knew right from the beginning, before he'd slept with either a man or a woman, that he wanted to be loved by a man, really loved. For Tom, homosexuality was not a primarily sexual fantasy, but a deeply emotional one, connected with desire as well as sex, and more inclusive than the sex that usually seemed to define homosexuality.

I suppose that this distinction between love and desire must also exist among heterosexuals—these different ways of wanting another person, the various kinds of lust and longing that may or may not complement each other, the potentially resulting hierarchies, the question of whether a person's wanting and wanting-to-possess and wanting-to-be-possessed are dominated by lust or love. Of course all that exists among heterosexuals too, but it often goes unnoticed because for them the discovery of desire is supposedly a one-off event and so much a matter of course that no one dares ask precisely what form the desire takes or what fuels it.

Looking back now, with hindsight, I have to rejig my experiences of that time. Today I would say that I, too, knew the longing that Tom felt, or at least a slight variation on the same theme—I wanted to be allowed to love other girls and women. And although I didn't recognise the lust within this deep longing, it was to surface again and again in my feelings for various women, most of them older than me; I just didn't ever associate it with the notion of homosexuality. I didn't even consciously associate it with 'love'.

Why not?

Perhaps if there had been references to lesbians somewhere in my everyday life, even condemnatory images or stories—anything at all, however crudely drawn—I might have managed to puzzle out my own behaviour and desires, the way Kossarinsky had taught us to listen to music, the way I had learnt to track down a motif and its permutations in a musical text. But to do that you had to know the theme, the original motif—you had to know what to listen out for.

It would have been even easier if I'd known a lesbian, someone who could have related to my longing. I wrote and wrote, naïvely and inefficiently courting the attention of girls and women, but I fell in love with boys and men who could certainly relate to my feelings for them. Tom, at least, knew that he wanted a man, although when he actually had a lover, a Syrian a few years older than him, he was at first surprised by the lust that accompanied this want. Over time, these different forms of longing would converge, his desire consolidate into a life.

Tom and I lost sight of each other for a few years, then bumped into each other on a train, only to lose touch again. We have recently reconnected. He's still as good looking as ever, and he still has the same floatiness that I found so infectious back then when I followed him up the steps to the Image.

—

At some point Daniel began to do worse at school. He had trouble concentrating, seemed absent and introspective, as if the outside were pushing him further and further inside himself, as if he couldn't get out into the world, into the books and texts that were supposed to prepare us for life. A blanket of gloom settled on him, wrapping him around, and he couldn't get out from underneath; it seemed to make everything harder for him—speaking, using his hands, gesturing.

Daniel had gone before he left us. He withdrew and nobody noticed. Or maybe people did notice, but everyone had got used to him being that way. He was isolated and lonely so no one was surprised when he became strange as well—strange, slower, more dull-witted.

The teachers had worried when Daniel had been ostracised, but it didn't occur to anyone that he might do worse academically as a result—that there might be a connection. Children from 'educationally disadvantaged' backgrounds, as they are called in today's euphemistic jargon, often had trouble at grammar schools—that fitted in with people's social prejudices and expectations, so nobody stopped to wonder whether this image of children from 'educationally disadvantaged backgrounds' wasn't perhaps itself to blame for their continuing educational struggles. No one looked for any other reason for Daniel's falling marks; no one considered the possibility of a link between puberty and isolation, loneliness and academic failure.

In the end, Daniel changed schools. He left the grammar school and went to the comprehensive a few bus stops away—another world. We didn't even say goodbye to him. The final sentence wasn't pronounced until reports were handed out on the last day of school. By then it was too late. We went off into the summer and Daniel, the steadily fading Daniel, disappeared.

In the autumn, at the beginning of the school year, when we moved into new classrooms, and Johannes and I could sit where we liked, I felt a sudden pang. Daniel, the boy we'd been asked to protect, the boy who had sat between us, was missing. Shame filled his place; there in the gap beside me, it made him more visible than he'd ever been before.

—

The boys' cruelty was shifting and erratic, varying from harmless to brutal. They went on the rampage whenever they felt the need to free their unsatisfied bodies from the isolation they'd forced themselves into, whenever they felt insecure about their masculinity. They went on the rampage, went hunting, hounding—someone who was worth it, no one too weak or helpless, no one too marginal; that would have been no fun; they'd have had no one to dominate, couldn't have proved themselves or demonstrated their power. Violence—that was what they needed, because only in violence towards others could they conceal their own predicament. When words failed them, there was always violence; it made it easier to lie, easier to conceal that cursed anxiety that never went away, no matter how many masculine coming-of-age rituals they put themselves through.

In order to be cruel to others—to beat them up and humiliate them—they sometimes needed alcohol: beer, vodka, whatever was available, whatever they could afford. Sometimes they needed to feel boredom—that helpless sense of not knowing where to put themselves. Sometimes it took an incident to spark things off—something that stirred up ancient, deep-seated emotions—a wrong word or gesture, old and familiar and painful. It only needed something that could be misconstrued as an invitation, so that the victim could be given the blame afterwards and everything could be denied: they hadn't done anything wrong; the violence wasn't violence, the humiliation wasn't humiliation—it was just a reflex, a bit of fun, a harmless joke.

And of course they'd all have said afterwards that it was only a game—no one had come to any harm, no one had got hurt. Micha had joined in; he'd even laughed. How could it be wrong when the boy in the middle of the circle had laughed? Didn't that prove that he'd had fun, that there was no cruelty involved? In fact, hadn't they done Micha a favour with their game? Wasn't it possible that he'd enjoyed being the centre of attention for once? Hadn't he had just as much fun as the others, at the end of the day?

There was no reason why Micha should have been singled out at the holiday camp that first evening; the boys had shown no signs of wanting to pick on him. Micha was good at school and popular, even if he tended to be some distance from the dominant centre, the inner clique. He was on the plump side and not very sporty, but he was always cheerful and happy and that gave him an air of invulnerability.

We'd spent the day on the beach and everyone ought to have been exhausted; there shouldn't have been any strength left in us that evening. All day long we'd played beach volleyball and been in and out of the surf. Maybe it wasn't enough. Maybe it was that last ounce of strength that was to blame. Or maybe it was the salt from the sea that had dried on our skin, making it prickle and itch so that back in the youth hostel that evening, everyone headed for the showers. Maybe something happened in the boys' showers that we girls didn't know about—at any rate, the next thing we knew, the boys were running after each other, their towels round their hips, their bare torsos still damp; they were laughing and clowning about, chasing around and trying to hit each other's bums with a wet towel. We could hear the slap of their wet feet and the smack when someone was hit.

It was harmless. It must have hurt, but still—it was a game, a bit like tag, only without a 'home' to run to. They slid over the slippery floor, half playful, half competitive, tottering along that narrow ridge between fun and anger, until somebody hit Micha—and Micha, being a bit clumsy, gave a little jump, like a scissor jump, pulling up first one leg, then the other, very quickly. Maybe it was just his awkwardness, maybe it was his fear; certainly the girly impression he made was aggravated by the fact that he squealed.

The boys stopped in their tracks. What was that?

Our teacher, Herr Paulsen, was standing at the end of the corridor. Did he want to show the boys how youthful he was? Or did he want to ingratiate himself with his athletic, bare-chested pupils? Whatever the reason, he came and joined the boys, slipping into a game that he should have put a stop to, and the next time the boys hit Micha—not just to inflict pain on him, but to see his little jump again—Paulsen only looked on with a mixture of surprise and enthusiasm—and laughed.

Micha didn't at first understand what had happened—why the boys had stopped running, why they weren't looking for another bum to whack, why they were coming to a standstill and forming a circle—a circle like on that first day of school, except that this time, instead of two people being pitted against each other, it was all against one, all against squealing Micha.

Paulsen looked on from the middle of the mob, and as the boys brought their wet towels down on Micha's bum with brisk, impulsive slaps, he suddenly cried out:

'Dance, Micha, dance!' Micha looked aghast into the slavering faces of the half-naked boys around him, laughing and jeering and hitting him—not too often, just enough to keep him jumping, to keep a rhythm going. Paulsen had provided them with a war cry and now they were all shouting: 'Dance, Micha, dance!' either because they really thought it funny or because they wanted to get in Paulsen's good books, and as they shouted, they took it in turns to hit Micha. Everyone got a go, everyone got to share in the fun, to get a kick out of the sense of power, the lack of restraint. Some of them probably shot their load in the process, some of them probably waited until later that night, back in their bunks, to wank out all the lust that Micha's humiliation had aroused in them.

And Micha danced, twisting and jumping up and down, squealing like a Russian circus bear tormented with a hot iron, who hopes the whip will soon drop so that it can get down from its idiotic ball. Red marks began to form on Micha's back. Now and then his pants slipped down and he frantically pulled them up, over the down in the hollow above his bum.

Those who weren't joining in stood around, forming a second circle, a circle of cowards surrounding the inner circle of Micha's tormentors. Some of them clapped; others grinned, amused or ashamed of themselves. They all knew things had gone too far—that Micha was suffering, that they were watching others get kicks out of humiliating him and making him suffer—but no one put a stop to it, no one wanted to step out of line or intervene. It would only have taken one person to divert attention from Micha, one person to grab hold of the towel. It would only have taken one person—and that person could have been *me*—to say that only wimps ganged up on a single person, that it was a game for boys with small dicks, for idiots—whatever. It would only have taken one person to say that it wasn't a game, wasn't funny.

I felt dizzy with disgust, standing there shuddering, a long way from both circles. I wish I could say I intervened. I wish I could say my dizziness made me as angry as I sometimes get today on my travels when I have to look on as people are maltreated or subjected to arbitrary power. I'd like to be able to say that I fetched Micha out of that circle and did a better job of protecting him than I did with Daniel, that I turned my revulsion to some use. But I can't. I have no act of bravery to report from that evening. Never again, I swore to myself the next day, never again would I look on speechlessly while that kind of thing was going on. And never again (I didn't even have to swear this to myself), never again would I trust circles, no matter how or why they were formed.

—

In my youth there were three places where I belonged, three places where I felt *right*, where I really fitted in:

the woods, the concert hall and the 'Front'. The woods
behind my parents' house had been my own private home
when I was little. After school, I would vanish into them,
not re-emerging until evening. At night, I could see the
treetops from my bed, and light shimmered through the
darkness to me from the hospital at the woods' edge.
I would run off to the woods whenever I felt unhappy,
and all my troubles seemed to melt away the moment I
breathed the smell of moss or heard the rustle of leaves.
Apart from a few blocks in New York, between Kenmare
Street, Houston Street, Sullivan Street and Elizabeth
Street, where I was trapped in the days following 9/11, I
know no place as well as those woods.

The concert hall was more regimented, full of rituals
I had to respect, but however severe and restrictive that
felt, the room seemed to expand in that magic moment
when the music started, opening up and opening *me* and
transcending everything else.

The Front was as reassuring as the woods, but for
different reasons. It was the only club I liked going to, even
if there was nothing inviting about the gloomy, bunker-
like vault. It was Tom who first took me there. Girls and
women were only allowed in the Front on Saturdays and
Wednesdays; the rest of the week, the club was 'men only'.
You usually had to queue, on the street outside, or on the
steps that led down past the bouncer to the cellar. It was
a run-down area; the Front was on a motorway slip road

and there wasn't much else round there except the vehicle registration office and dosshouses for truckers. These days, it's mainly refugees living there, officially or otherwise, in those bleak buildings on the edge of town.

Inside, the walls were pale grey and there was almost nothing in the way of fittings or furniture; it was an unadorned cellar of steel and bare concrete, with a cloakroom behind a grille, a functional bar and gay porn projected onto a video wall. What mattered was the music. The DJ cabin was made of tinted plexiglas and you couldn't see in from the outside. The Cologne DJ Klaus Stockhausen spun here on two Thorens TD524 and a Technics 1210 MK11; later Boris Dlugosch took over. I didn't know that at the time; it wouldn't have interested me. What I did know was that nowhere else did they mix music like at the Front—nowhere else was there this ecstatic atmosphere, this endless dancing.

The Front was established in 1983 by Willi Prange and his partner Phillip Clarke. When asked for his political views in an interview, Prange once replied: 'I'm a foreigner.' And that's a little how it felt; I was a foreigner at the Front, which made me right at home in that place where you could be if you didn't fit in or belong anywhere else. There was also a lesbian disco, the 'Camelot', but it didn't appeal to me. The Front was Tom's club and it made me happy to see how happy he was there, where his homosexuality was, if not irrelevant, then at least nothing unusual—and where the stigma and burden of being a loner fell away from him (from us both).

It was cramped and stuffy in the Front. The only light came from coloured neon lights and a DANGER lamp or two. I don't think there was a dark room, but I probably wouldn't have known. All I wanted was to dance for hours to the booming beats, surrounded by slender-limbed transgender people and half-naked leather gays. At first there were even a few mods—everything mingled; all the differences that were so important outside, in the light of day, in the other world, were irrelevant here. It gave me an endless sense of freedom.

We went there week after week. It was like travelling to another country; the nights at the Front transported us to another world that knocked the established order out of action. What was special about the Front was that it was nothing special to be gay there. The attraction wasn't that everyone was the same (i.e. gay), but that sameness and difference played no part.

Even today when I return to Berlin from a not particularly homophile country and go to my favourite bar in Kreuzberg, that same feeling of happiness comes over me, the same sense of relief that I can just *be*, that I don't have to be anyone else or cause offence or stick out as unusual, that I can kiss another woman—that I can be all over another woman, and no one will care or even notice. There's something cathartic about it, especially after the troubles and constraints of the countries where I go to research. Being back from one of those trips is always liberating, every time.

Phillip Clarke died of cancer in 2003; his boyfriend Willi Prange took his life in 2006. Today, Front revival parties are held every four years and there are minidisc recordings in circulation. Although the club no longer exists, those of us who danced the nights away there have never lost that feeling of having a place—that sense of a home, where everyone could be a foreigner and the never-ending exile came to an end. No one has ever been able to take that from us. Today the 'meschugge' parties in Berlin's Mitte or the 'GayHane' nights in Kreuzberg where DJ Ipek spins perhaps come closest to what the Front was to us back then.

—

My literary world at that time was a wild mix of prescribed reading—Maupassant and the Goethe of *Wilhelm Meister's Apprenticeship*, Flaubert and the Goethe of *The Sorrows of Young Werther*, Max Frisch and the Goethe of *Elective Affinities*, Thomas Mann and the Goethe of *Faust*—and of reading that found me by other routes: Albert Camus and Jean-Paul Sartre, Hölderlin and Georg Büchner, Paul Celan and Wolfgang Koeppen, Christa Wolf and Ernst Bloch. Apart from the inevitable Jane Austen in our rather uninspired English lessons, I can't remember there being a single female author on the syllabus. No Virginia Woolf, no Simone de Beauvoir, no Joan Didion or Carson McCullers—let alone Hannah Arendt or Ingeborg Bachmann. Female thinkers, female narrative voices were a rarity, in literature and philosophy.

If you wanted to identify with heroes in films, you had to identify with men. Female role models were few and far between. Women—such was the message of the old genre films that were still being shown on television—were confused hysterical creatures languishing in the country, who spent most of the film waiting to marry the wrong man and then fell in love with Mr Right at the eleventh hour; they were large-breasted saloon ladies who'd seen better days, feverishly awaiting the return of John Wayne, or chaste long-haired chatelaines who would, in the end, be liberated by Robert Taylor, but not until he'd seized Jerusalem or knocked several heavyweight knights off their horses with his lance.

From an early age I was an expert at identifying with active (male) characters. Of course I was Winnetou—who wanted to be Nscho-tschi, when it meant waiting months for Winnetou's return, missing out on all the adventures and then dying, faint-voiced, in his arms? If you wanted to imagine yourself into the role of an active character, you had as a rule to watch the films of that time from the male perspective—leaving yourself with little choice but to fall in love with whichever woman your hero fell for. Looking back, I find it impossible to say whether I imagined myself into the male personae so that I could fall in love with the women, or whether I fell in love with the women because I wanted to be the active, dynamic character. I never wanted to be a man; I just wanted to be free.

If I'd gone to the theatre in my schooldays, to the Schauspielhaus where Peter Zadek was director, I would have seen more Eva Mattes and Susanne Lothar. If I'd known the films of Fassbinder, I would have been familiar with other narrative forms and ways of living. But at the time I knew nothing of any other visual language or alternative female characters.

The great female roles that came later—thinking and self-assured women whose point of view was at last central to the story—were often tragic figures, troubled and full of pain, and by then I'd got so used to thinking myself into the male roles that I wanted to be Alain Delon or Sami Frey and was in love with Romy Schneider. The split into male and female characters was more than just a split into male and female; linked to the characters were images that were only ever conferred on one group or the other—images of happiness or power, images of powerlessness and suffering.

This aesthetic and existential order shattered in a single evening when my mother took me to the opening night of a Harry Kupfer production of Handel's *Belshazzar* at the State Opera House. I still didn't like opera, but

I loved Baroque music and she knew I'd recognise the Bible stories: the Jews in Babylonian captivity, the Feast of Sesach, the mysterious writing on the wall, the prediction that Nebuchadnezzar's kingdom would fall—she guessed I'd like all that. It must have been soon before I left school.

When the voice first rang out, I couldn't move. I froze in my seat in the back row of a box level with the dress circle, listening to a counter tenor for the first time in my life:

> *Lament not thus, o Queen, in vain!*
> *Virtue's part is to resign*
> *All things to the will divine,*
> *Nor of its just decrees complain.*
> *The sins of Babylon urge on her fate;*
> *But virtue still this comfort gives,*
> *On earth she finds a safe retreat,*
> *Or bless'd in Heav'n for ever lives.*
> *Lament not thus...*

I'd never heard anything like it. That voice seemed to transcend everything I knew, everything that had previously held good. It seemed to float, disembodied, elusive, beyond gender.

I followed every movement of that slender figure. I knew and loved the story of the boy who can interpret dreams, the boy who recalls the predictions of Isaiah

and Jeremiah, and can read the writing on the wall—
mene mene tekel upharsin: numbered, weighed (and found
wanting), divided—the boy who speaks the truth that
the others are afraid to speak—can't speak. He seems to
move in the cracks of the story. If it had been a ballet,
Max Midinet would have danced the character of Daniel.
That evening, the part was sung by Jochen Kowalski and
that of Nictoris by Helen Donath, and every aria I heard
was another rip in a heavy curtain that until then had
concealed all possibilities of sound.

The production, too, bowled me over. To the audience's horror, Harry Kupfer had set the story of the Jewish
people in a ghetto, but as I saw it, that only gave the role of
Daniel a sense of greater urgency. I looked forward to each
of his appearances with nervous anticipation, anxious to
move closer to the resolution of that unsettling story, but
more than that, desperate to hear a voice that seemed to
soar above all other sounds, all other groups and peoples
and choirs. I went home a different person.

Years later, I was similarly stirred when I saw Corinna
Harfouch raging and rampaging in the part of General
Harras, in Frank Castorf's production of *The Devil's
General* at the Volksbühne. Her performance played
havoc with identification and desire, making everything
come alight; in the ambivalence of a female actor playing
a male role, fury and doubt and passion seemed to flicker
in and out of view like figures in a picture puzzle. Corinna

Harfouch didn't strip the character of his physicality like the counter tenor; she made him *not* sexless, deploying all her physicality and sensuality to break down received notions of masculinity and femininity. She seemed to interweave masculine and feminine until they were indistinguishable, leaving me with a confused, unsettling and thrilling pleasure that continued to resonate long after the play was over and I had gone home.

I met her not long ago. Friends in Berlin had invited Corinna Harfouch to their wedding and luckily I was drunk enough to pluck up the courage to speak to her. I didn't want to repeat the mistake of shy silence I had made with Max Midinet. Stammering slightly, I told her about my evening at the Volksbühne and that it had been one of those rare moments when a work of art changes your life. I think she was pleased.

—

'Modulation' is a term in harmony that denotes the transition from one key to another. Perhaps this compositional technique of major-minor tonality is also the best way to describe what was happening back then—what Daniel, Tom and I were going through, but also what countless others, homosexual or not, still experience today: that desire can develop and even change, that various forms of desire can exist in parallel, that one person can, at different times, feel quite different forms of lust and longing, some of which are fulfilled, while others will only ever be hinted at, that the sound of our lives isn't governed from beginning to end by a single norm, but that the source key really is just that—a source, a beginning, a first desire, a first sound that can later develop into something quite different.

In music you speak of 'modulation' when a piece begins in one key—to which the ear accustoms itself harmonically—and then shifts into another. Some pieces of music switch key without warning, without harmonic preparation, without intermediary notes to suggest a possible change of key. Music theory calls this 'abrupt modulation'. Usually, though, transitional steps—notes or chords that no longer belong to the tonic—announce a shift. Sometimes, chords are ambivalent because they could be interpreted as belonging to either key. That is true modulation.

Today I realise that I must have sounded like a long-announced modulation in those days. A well-trained listener would have been able to point to notes suggesting a later shift in key; as it was, it took me years to find my way to desiring differently. Much about me must have seemed alien or at least ambivalent: my love of sport, my nights at the Front, my friendship with Tom. I sought the attention of women—but I fell in love with men.

Perhaps that way I was able to appropriate spaces for myself, to find the freedom to deviate from expectations, to experiment with different forms and languages, and play with variations on the norm, as I had learnt in music. Perhaps there was no harmonic goal; perhaps the alien-sounding notes or chords in me could just as easily have retained their ambivalence and remained unresolved. Or perhaps they were the beginning of my developing desire.

Why had no one told us that desire can shift like a musical key—that a source key, an initial form of lust can develop into another and sometimes yet another? Why isn't this something people talk about? Why is sexuality deprived of its playful, light-hearted, dynamic side? Why are the tones and keys of lust seen in such static, limited, one-sided terms? Why doesn't modulation play a part in the way we think about desire?

Of course, just as different keys have chords in common, different forms of desire share certain practices or gestures. Just as some tones belong to one key or another, certain feelings or signs can appear ambivalent; they can be embedded in a homosexual or heterosexual story, a male or female one. Perhaps that's what made it so hard for me and those who knew me to be clear about whether my desire would shift.

How often does it happen that we meet someone and have the feeling that all the signs point the same way? We look at someone and interpret all the codes and gestures we see as indications of a sexuality that isn't actually lived by that person, that doesn't (yet) correspond with his or her self-perception. Sometimes we meet a young person and think: that girl sounds as if she'll be a man one day. The possibility of a sex change is in the air. Sometimes the sound fades and comes to nothing; at other times the harmonic goal is reached. In some cases the girl will become a man; in others she won't. Sometimes a variety of keys are hinted at, but everything ends up returning to the tonic.

Perhaps I needed those common chords to help me discover my desire. In diatonic modulation, chords that are shared by two or more keys have a transitional function, easing the shift from one key to another. Perhaps it's the same with us; perhaps we need certain forms of lust or sexuality in order to arrive at others. That needn't only apply to a shift in the object of sexuality—whether someone desires men or women; perhaps the subjectivity of our desire needs similar transitions to develop; perhaps certain familiar chords—certain familiar sexual practices—suddenly feel different, suddenly arouse us in a different way.

Perhaps what's special about puberty is that it's a time when all these modulations of desire and individuality seem possible because there's such great uncertainty and ambivalence; it's a time when many of us let slip incongruous notes that don't belong to the given tonic. Some people have no harmonic goal; some shift tone many times over, others never; some will retain an ambivalent tone for the rest of their lives. In some people the transition is abrupt—unannounced and unprepared; in others, like me, the transitional period can go on for years.

The first woman I knew to sleep with women was also the first woman I slept with. By then I was twenty-five. As soon as the possibility was real and I met my first beautiful bisexual woman, I desperately wanted to touch her, to love her, to *have* her. Perhaps—though I can only speculate—I would have slept with a woman at sixteen, if I'd met one who desired women earlier.

I remember the first time I saw her, really saw her, and thought: 'How beautiful she is.' Only that what I actually thought was: 'She's so beautiful all the men must be crazy about her.' I looked at her, watching the way she sat and spoke and crossed her legs, following her every movement, her every gesture. I wanted to touch her— touch her hands and lips and legs—but I thought men must think that; I didn't think the thought as my own. That must be the way men look at women, I thought—the way they think about them and desire them; it reached me only through a heterosexual filter. I interpreted my situation in terms of the social context familiar to me: this was the kind of attraction that existed between men and women; it was the way I usually looked at men.

Like the women in Gaza who couldn't see the woman in me because there weren't women like me in their social milieu, I couldn't recognise the gaze that desired as my own because I hadn't—until then—desired women. It wasn't that I'd banned myself from wanting women. I hadn't censored my feelings because I thought them wrong or perverse; it was just that the taboo was so firmly internalised that it had swallowed or displaced my desire even before I had realised it was mine.

It was only when I couldn't stop looking at her—when the attraction grew too urgent to ignore, that I finally recognised the lustful gaze as my own: *I desired a woman.* To this day that astounds me. Not that I became homosexual, but that it took me so long to work it out—that I didn't spot the signs earlier, that I failed to hear all those notes suggesting modulation. Even in that first instant, when I realised I was falling in love with a woman, I was surprised at my own slowness. Why hadn't I noticed earlier? How was it possible? Was it even possible? For years, after all, I'd loved only men.

I don't know if the desire was there all along and only needed triggering. I don't know what finally awoke it or why it found expression in me when it did. Other people's homosexuality is unambiguous from the outset; they know they aren't able or willing to desire or love any other way. Maybe all it took was for me to meet a woman who desired women. Maybe I needed all those years with men, all those different bodies and their different ways of loving. Maybe I needed time and another form of sexuality to find my way deeper and deeper into my own desire. Maybe after a while it wasn't so much I who determined my lust as my lust that determined me and I abandoned myself to helpless desire, as if to an all-consuming force.

It is often assumed that women become homosexual because they aren't comfortable having sex with men. It's true that many lesbians are clear all along about their homosexuality; they desire women and never have an interest in the opposite sex. In my case, though, I think it was eroticism with men which, precisely *because* it gave me pleasure, opened the way to the greater and more exciting desire for women. Perhaps heterosexual eroticism acted like a chord that is common to two keys; perhaps it was the cadence that led me to a new key, a new subjectivity of desire.

That is, I suspect, not so very unusual. There are women who find their way to men via sex with women, when they discover that sex with a dildo gives them pleasure; there are women who discover with men that they like sex without penetration; there are men who only want to sleep with women the way they could sleep with men; heterosexual men who are aroused by lesbian porn; gay men married to women—the variations are endless. Sometimes the object of desire is less important than the nature of the desire. It isn't only who we desire that matters, but also *how* we desire—not a specific note or chord, but where in the music it comes. Even the partner's sex can be of little importance or relevance for deep, unrestrained arousal and lust.

It took a little while of hesitant courtship before we found each other, but the feeling was so irrefutable and unequivocal—a feeling of such deep lust that I was desperate to love her. There was no longer any doubt that I desired. Maybe that was one difference between this desire and the way I had desired men: this unconditional want—not just being wanted, but feeling the longing myself, having the space to develop my desire for this body, being able to watch myself desiring. Never before had I felt that so intensely; it surpassed all previous forms of lust and longing.

What aroused me so much about women, and still affects me deeply to this day, was (and is) the lack of certainty: not knowing whether the other woman also wants me, not knowing whether the gamble will pay off, whether my efforts will come to anything. That I have to make an effort at all, that I have to put myself out, that there's a chance that the woman I want might *not* find me exciting or beautiful or desirable—all that uncertainty, so necessary for desire and longing to flourish, was (and is) overwhelming.

The first time I fell in love with a woman, I had no doubt about either my feelings or my desire to pursue them. I was only unsure whether I'd manage—whether I might not turn out to be a clumsy and inexperienced lover (and it's true there was a grotesque moment when I couldn't undo her bra and wished I could do it backwards, as if it were my own). I was afraid, too—afraid I might not like it and would reject her, and afraid I'd like it so much that I'd have to devalue or dismiss all my experiences with men. I didn't want to lose my past with this new experience. I didn't want to have to reinterpret as meaningless the exciting and beautiful times I'd had with men.

All I wanted back then was this one particular woman. I didn't stop to wonder, in the first rush of desire, whether that meant I would be wanting all the other women who desire women, whether I'd be part of an identity group. It wasn't that I didn't like lesbians or that they were unsympathetic to me; I just didn't want to be a member of a club. All I wanted was to sleep with this woman.

After a while, though, after the first night and the first day and all the other days and nights, as my desire only grew and I loved my way deeper and deeper, the question eventually reared its head: who would I be if I stopped loving men and suddenly only loved women? What difference would it make? Would it make a difference? Did I want it to? Did I feel any different?

My first instinct was to say: *It makes no difference at all.* Why should it? Why should my desire alone determine who I was? Why should it make any difference who I slept with, who I came for? Why was it relevant to my life? Why should it interfere with my thoughts, my writing, my work, my friends? Wasn't it up to me how much my lust ruled my life?

Was it my 'nature'? Was it innate? Did I have to love women from now on? It's true, the desire was spreading through me with such urgency that I really had no choice, but I also wanted it—I wanted to *live* this lust, not just once, in secret, but openly and many times; I didn't want it to be a passing thing; I wanted it to overwhelm me and stay. I know that declaring homosexuality immutable and innate rather than a matter of choice is a strategy sometimes employed—a response to those who want to ban homosexuality and 're-educate' homosexuals, as if we had a speech impediment—but I've never liked that variation on biologistic self-disenfranchisement that declares homosexuality nature rather than nurture, making of nature a kind of shield that you hold before you.

Of course, homosexual desire may be genetically conditioned; I don't doubt that some people have a natural disposition to homosexuality. But I'm not queer simply because nature has decided to make me that way— because I'm incapable of being any different. I am also queer because it makes me happy, because I *want* to love my way into women, because it feels right and because I decided on this way of loving all those years ago, when I first saw a woman and wanted her—when I wanted her body and her desire and realised I couldn't get enough.

'Home is where we start from,' the psychoanalyst D.

W. Winnicott once said, and it is no more and no less than that. It is where we begin, where we set off from. It's not where we stay; it's not somewhere that accompanies us unchanged. When we set off on our wanderings in pursuit of our desire, we are driven by a restlessness and a sense of exile to search for another home, another home-land. The first time I slept with a woman—and the second and the third—I had arrived.

I now know that I didn't have to reinterpret or devalue my earlier experiences; the lust I had felt with men remained the lust I had felt with men. But it was only the beginning. The lust I feel when I sleep with a woman is more intense, the desire more overwhelming than anything else, perhaps because it's less circumscribed and thus less certain, perhaps because my own lust, the way I love my way into another woman, another body, is less self-evident, more open. I feel freer being able to sound out the other woman's lust searchingly, tentatively, with my lips or hands or all my body, when there is no centre and no periphery—when everything seems possible and I am able and allowed to be everything in my lust, free of preconceptions about the meaning of 'lustful', 'feminine', 'arousing' or 'forbidden', free of all doubt and protection, unrestrained and vulnerable, beside myself and in myself at the same time.

And it hasn't let up since. It has deepened, intensified, acquired clearer outlines—I suppose because, through my sexuality, I myself and my life have also acquired clearer outlines.

—

I sometimes saw Daniel after he'd left our school—in the pub where everyone met to drink and play billiards, or down by the river. Now that he was at the comprehensive, he had a *Krad*, a small motorbike—maybe to help him make the longer journey to school, maybe to make it easier for him to lend a hand at the nursery and get to customers' gardens under his own steam. Sometimes, when the sun was setting, he'd turn up at the river on this motorbike, park it and walk down to the shore. He had new friends—or acquaintances. You couldn't tell from the outside whether he'd found a clique. Were the boys he hung out with his friends? Did he felt comfortable with them? Or was he simply glad not to be excluded any more?

We greeted each other, usually from a distance, smiling and shy, as if we were strangers but would like to get to know one another. And in a way that was true.

—

Then sexuality began to be associated with death. The first news of the as yet little-known epidemic AIDS (still spelt 'A.I.D.S.' in those days)[46] came to us from the United States. In 1983 the *Spiegel*, and journalist Hans Halter in particular, started to report on the 'epidemic' that was 'only just beginning', spreading fear of the illness that would be described as a 'sickness unto death'.

Everything was unclear. What united this cluster of disparate symptoms? Was it an illness in its own right, or merely a condition that facilitated the outbreak of other illnesses? How was it transmitted? Only one thing seemed certain in this welter of ignorance: it affected 'the others'. AIDS helped separate 'us' from 'them'—'we' being women or faithful heterosexual men, while 'the others' were sex-crazed gay men and drug addicts. 'We', the first reports and discussions suggested, would be spared; AIDS, the 'pink plague', was reputedly a gay disease.

Whatever had once kept homosexuality shrouded in invisibility—shame or taboo, censorship or repression, discretion or fear—it was now over. Homosexual lust was suddenly no longer hushed up; instead, with a mixture of moralising horror and unrestrained schadenfreude, the sexual practices of homosexual men were expounded on and appraised.

Writing in the *Spiegel* in June 1983, Hans Halter quoted Berlin bacteriologist Professor Franz Fehrenbach. When asked whether and why homosexual men were at risk of infection, Fehrenbach replied that perhaps 'the Lord always [had] a scourge ready for homosexuals'.[47]

The reports on AIDS transformed gay men— until then, little-known figures who'd had to live their desire surreptitiously and in isolation—into hordes of promiscuous nymphomaniacs who held wild orgies in clubs and saunas and blindly threw themselves at each other. And suddenly people were talking about sex. Always, it is true, in morally derogatory tones, always in connection with epidemic risk, always in terms of the 'impure', the sick and the threatening—but still, people were talking about sexual practices in more detail than would ever have been thought possible, certainly in our world, at our school.

Suddenly, terms like 'anal intercourse', 'ejaculated semen' and 'mucous membrane' were common parlance, and people thought nothing of referring to the organs and practices of 'blithely swinging homosexuals' (Halter) in their discussions of 'gay lust' and the medical causes of the infection. If the strategy behind this debate was to reduce homosexual lust to something abhorrent, I suspect I wasn't the only one to remain unconvinced. Perhaps one reason was that the heterosexual writers had a tendency to sound envious in spite of themselves. An example from 1984:

> Maybe it's easier to understand why so many queers don't (or can't) stop their promiscuous carry-ings-on, if we imagine, just in our minds, similar sexual freedom for straight people: no more registry office, no marriage certificate—instead, jacuzzis and champagne and a relaxation room full of beautiful girls to choose between. A flirt in a dark night and you move on.[48]

Reading this, you think: poor heterosexual author, wanting to imagine 'just in his mind' what it would be like to be 'free'—although how else you'd go about imagining things, if not in your mind, is something of a mystery. Quite apart from that, though, the whole idea of a gay life consisting entirely of 'jacuzzis and champagne' is preposterous.

People told bad jokes about AIDS. Mathematicians embarked on statistical calculations quantifying sex in order to chart the spread of disease and predict worst-case scenarios. There were fantasies of quarantine zones for those infected, and the old metaphor resurfaced of the 'healthy body politic' and its need for protection.

I don't know what impact the public debate would have had on me if I hadn't known Tom. I don't know whether the newly drawn order would have convinced me: safe heterosexuals on the one hand, threatened homosexuals on the other; straightforward, healthy sex here, sick and diseased sex over there. Maybe I'd have been more likely to accept the boundary that, since the emergence of AIDS, was being redrawn daily.

But Tom was my friend, and he didn't grow more alien or more threatening, but closer; now that he seemed more vulnerable, we only grew nearer. I wasn't afraid of him; I was afraid *for* him. We still went out together; we went on weekend trips to Berlin and danced the night away in Linientreu, and together we discovered the music of Bronski Beat with Jimmy Somerville.

I'm sure it wasn't intentional, but those early debates on AIDS played an important part in shaping my ideas about what friends are for. Friendship was tied up with the notion of care, and possibly final care—that wasn't necessary in Tom's case, but all the stories coming from the USA suggested that we were going to have to look after each other ourselves. In 1984, the US President Ronald Reagan still hadn't even mentioned the word 'AIDS'. Edward N. Brandt Jr., an assistant secretary of Health and Human Services, announced that there was no need for panic because there were no indications that the epidemic was 'breaking out from the originally defined high-risk groups'. [49] In other words: as long as gays, junkies and Haitians were the only ones affected, there was no cause for concern.

> Homosexuals are often called on not to neglect their sick; they themselves accept the obligation in their days of health, and—to the amazement of the doctors treating them—they keep their word.[50]

I wasn't homosexual, Tom wasn't infected with HIV and yet the circle was closing around us and for the first time it felt like a form of protection. We would protect each other—like a family, but a family of our own choosing, made up of friends rather than relations. Later, when it became clear that it wasn't just gay men who were affected, but everyone—that haemophiliacs and other blood recipients, heterosexual men and women and children were also at risk—this sense of friendship and family remained unchanged.

—

The boy was lying in a steel cot, scratching himself. On the left of his forehead, from the ear up, a semi-circular scar bulged like a shrivelled appendix, and a white, blotchy fungus spread over his dark head to his neck. In some places, scabs had formed, making greyish clumps out of his thin hair. This seven-month-old baby had been found the night before outside a police station in Meru, in eastern Kenya. Someone had abandoned the little thing; he was clearly unwanted. Maybe his mother didn't want a sick child or a child with HIV. Maybe it was too expensive to care for a creature that was going to die anyway. Maybe the sight of the baby repelled her. Maybe he no longer had a mother, but only a grandmother. Maybe.

The doctors had called the child Trevor and given him antibiotics for a streptococcus infection. Now baby Trevor was lying on a green rubber mattress and a thin woollen blanket in a big, dirty room, scratching his head bloody. Next to him a little girl with dark wavy hair was standing in her cot gripping the rail, so as to get a better view of what was going on around her.

The two-year-old girl with the huge watchful eyes had

been on the children's ward of Meru General Hospital for a week. Someone had abandoned her not far from there. Unlike Trevor, the little girl wasn't sick. Unlike Trevor she didn't have HIV; the doctors had examined her. The only thing wrong with her was that she was completely deaf; she couldn't hear the television set on the wall where the nurses watched soap operas, or the rattle of bars in the cot next to her that was occupied by an almost fully grown boy with cerebral palsy. Maybe her mother hadn't wanted a deaf child. Maybe the girl had lived with her father, and her new stepmother hadn't known what to do with her, so she'd been thrown out, like rotten fruit.

'Children don't count here,' said Dr Felix Oindi, the paediatrician on the children's ward. 'Everything else comes first.' And so the ward was full of unwanted children—babies who'd been thrown into public latrines, battered children, neglected or abused children, sick, injured, healthy children.

We'd spent a week shadowing a local organisation that rescues children from their own families: boys whose fathers attack them with machetes, eleven-year-old girls who are pregnant by their neighbours or their own grandfathers, HIV-positive babies who get hurt because they're regarded as useless and too expensive, four-year-olds who are raped by their landlord, girls who are afraid of being abused again, forced to run away because the stigma of abuse marks the victims, not the offenders.

We'd spent a week watching the desperate search for families willing to take in these children who aren't protected by the law—and one evening, the day we'd been to the hospital and seen Trevor, I asked whether I couldn't adopt one of these children.

The answer was plain and clear: homosexuality was illegal in Kenya. Someone like me didn't have a chance of getting a child.

A dozen children are lying on that ward, vegetating—babies and toddlers, HIV-positive or deaf; sick, handicapped or healthy; children nobody wants, children no one can feed or love, and whose only hope (because there aren't enough families to take them in) is that they'll be passed from home to home. A dozen children—and none of them could come with me because I'm illegal? None of them could live with me because I'm homosexual? How much more damaging than all that those children have been through can my homosexuality be?

Strictly speaking it's more complicated. Kenyan law only prohibits male homosexuality. Women aren't even mentioned. The question is, then, whether something that doesn't exist de jure—a lesbian couple—can adopt a child de facto. If I really wanted a child, I could always lie, my photographer suggested—but I don't want to lie in order to be able to adopt a child; I don't want to have to pretend to be single. Firstly because I'm not, and secondly because I can't see why it should be better for a child to be brought up by a single mother than by two mothers.

The idea that homosexuals shouldn't adopt children is not restricted to Kenya. In Germany, too, homosexual couples are barred from adopting other people's children. The SPD-Green coalition government went as far as legalising 'stepchild adoption', extending the Civil Partnership Act (so called only to avoid the word 'marriage') to allow homosexuals to adopt the biological children of their partners as of 1 January 2005. But while gay and lesbian couples in Andorra, Argentina, Belgium, Denmark, the UK, Iceland, Ireland, the Netherlands, Norway, Sweden, Spain and South Africa can also adopt other people's children, it remains illegal in Germany.[51]

When in summer 2009 the minister of justice, Social Democrat Brigitte Zypries, suggested that homosexual couples be given full adoption rights, Volker Kauder of the CDU replied: 'This proposal is all about the self-realisation of lesbians and gays; it has nothing to do with the wellbeing of the children.'

Perhaps it's a good thing that Kauder voiced an opinion that is usually restricted to the middle-class kitchen table and choked back in public. At least it makes it possible to answer.

Why shouldn't we be allowed to adopt children? Herr Kauder makes it sound as if self-realisation were reprehensible. But for what reasons do heterosexual couples have children? And why should self-realisation be incompatible with the wellbeing of a child? Who defines that anyway—a child's wellbeing?

Why, in a country that is always invoking the Enlightenment and secularisation, are there laws that seem committed to the anti-Enlightenment? Why, in a country that proclaims equality before the law, are there still laws enshrining inequality? Why do we have to keep defining *who* is equal—not just men, but also women and transsexuals; not just Christians, but also Jews and Muslims and Roma; not just believers of a different faith, but also non-believers? Why isn't it enough to say that all people are equal before the law? Why, when we have declared human dignity inviolable, does it end up being violable pro re nata for non-whites, non-heterosexuals, non-Christians, non-men? Why must it take us decades to be clear about who counts as human?

Why is marriage regarded as sacred and inviolable, but not the people who want to come together in marriage? Why can't the same form of attachment always have the same name? Why can homosexuals only be 'partnered' and not 'married'?[52] Why are there still laws forbidding us from adopting children? Why are there still rights reserved for heterosexuals? Why can't marriage simply be open to those who want it, with all its rights and responsibilities, regardless of whether a couple is heterosexual or homosexual? It would be a simple legal act. Spain has shown it can be done.

The facts are remarkable. On average, more than half of all civil marriages and families break up. According to the Federal Statistical Office, there were 378,439 marriages in 2009 and 185,817 divorces. Birth rates are low; journalists and politicians regularly evoke the dangers of demographic developments and in 2010 the number of deaths surpassed the number of births by 180,821. But marriage as an institution continues to be restricted to heterosexual couples, and protected by law from alleged corruption, as if homosexuals wanting to marry were more of a threat to marriage than heterosexuals filing for divorce. Wanting to adopt children is regarded as 'self-realisation' in homosexuals—and yet people complain about the lack of children in Germany.

I admit I'm not sure what best serves a child's well-being. I'm as uncertain as everyone who doesn't have children, and maybe even as uncertain as those who *do*. The task of raising a child seems to me an extraordinary blessing and a considerable responsibility. I don't know if I'd always be able to muster the right combination of patience and impatience, if I'd be as good as my brother at striking the balance between challenging and protecting a child, or as wonderful a mother as my own mother, who knew how to love unconditionally and at the same time how to let go. I don't know if I'd allow my child to get up to all the same nonsense I was allowed to get up to—if she wouldn't, like me, end up thinking her mother annoying, conservative and too strict. In fact, that's the one thing I am sure of—she would think me annoying, conservative and too strict.

I admit that a family seems to me a risky business, no matter what kind of family it is—two mothers, or a father and a grandmother. It has always seemed strange to me that such a complex structure should pass for the most natural thing in the world, that it should pass for so easy, when it never was—not for our parents and not for our grandparents either. It's as if the stories of hurt didn't exist; as if all those secrets and lies had never been—all the pain and loss that is passed down from generation to generation, the burden weighing on us all.

But why shouldn't I be allowed to try? Why shouldn't homosexuals have the chance to believe in this happiness? Why should wanting a child arouse suspicions? What's reprehensible about such a desire?

Not only are homosexual couples not allowed to adopt children together; artificial insemination by donor sperm from a sperm bank is also tricky for gay couples in Germany—unlike in the USA, Denmark or Israel, for example. Doctors who carry out this form of 'assisted reproduction' do so in contravention of guidelines from the German Medical Association. While heterosexual couples who are unable to have children can fulfil their desire for children through 'heterologous' or artificial insemination by an anonymous donor, the German

Medical Association explicitly rules out this possibility for lesbian couples in its comments on the guidelines on 'assisted reproduction',[53] which argue that women who do not live in a partnership, or who live in a homosexual partnership are at present barred from using assisted reproduction because they cannot guarantee a stable two-parent relationship for their children.

That is absurd. A (lesbian) couple seeking IVF are clearly two people who want to become parents—the parents of a child that the biological mother's partner will be able to adopt as her stepchild.[54] But because of the legal uncertainty, doctors in Germany who use assisted reproduction to help lesbian couples conceive risk losing their licence to practise.

Why aren't we allowed access to IVF? Why are 'nature' and 'naturalness' treated as clearly irrelevant when heterosexual couples want to conceive—why can medical reproductive technology come to their help as a matter of course, while the same technology is denied to homosexual couples wanting a child? Now that we're officially allowed to love the way we love at last, why shouldn't we be allowed to bear and raise children? Because that would mean challenging the sacred institution of marriage and the bourgeois family? But what exactly defines the bourgeois family? The individuals or the conventions? The manliness of the men and the femininity of the women? That wasn't even true of the Buddenbrooks.

Such families have de facto existed for a long time. We are surrounded by the children of our gay and lesbian friends; adopted or biological, they grow up with us, and our friends worry about them just as all parents or care-givers worry about their children. When I think of the kids we know—of Furio or Viva, Ben or Isaac, I think about how crumpled they looked when they were first born, think of them relentlessly dribbling all over their dads' smart shirts or learning to ski with their mums, of the photos taken on their first days at school or at their bar mitzvahs. I don't think about where they come from, whether the insemination was artificial or natural, or whether their beaming parents are gay or lesbian.

There are children who have two mothers and an anonymous father from a sperm bank whom they'll never know. There are children who have a mother and two fathers—a gay couple, one of whom is the biological father. There are children who have two mothers who live together and a father who can see his son or daughter as often as he likes. Some fathers are ex-boyfriends. Some are gay, some heterosexual. Some prefer to remain anonymous, others want to play a part in their children's lives, either as fatherly friends or as fathers—and, most importantly, almost all the grandparents are dying to be grandparents.

Of course this is new. It's new that a man looks for a woman to be the mother of his child without wanting to be her lover, or that a woman looks for a father for her child without wanting to be *his* lover. We aren't used to thinking about parenthood as distinct from the relationship between two people. But don't you get the same thing in heterosexual couples and families, only on a less public level? How many children do I know who don't know their fathers and are growing up with just their mum? How many children have parents who are no longer together? And how many men choose a woman on the basis of whether they can imagine her as the mother of their children? Is it really so very different?

What is different is that we can't have unplanned children. We have to think about whether we want children, and, if so, how we want to have them. That means confronting yourself with questions that sound strangely rational, although they end up forming a finely spun web of emotions: do I mind whether my child is biologically related to me or not? Do I want to get pregnant or adopt? If I decide to adopt, does it matter what part of the world the child comes from? Am I being biologistic? Am I being racist? Would I rather have a child from Vietnam than from Kenya? Why? If I decide to get pregnant (by an anonymous donor or a friend who agrees to act as the father or donor), what would that mean for my partner who would be raising a child who wasn't related to her? I can dismiss all these questions—but I can't stop them from coming.

I once went through all the possibilities. I didn't know if I really wanted a child, but I was approaching my late thirties and I knew I *had* to go through the options because it would soon be too late. I wanted to know if I *could* have a child and I wanted to know how. I decided that if I did, I'd like to give birth to it myself. So I'd need a father. Sperm donation from an anonymous sperm bank abroad was out of the question for me. I have friends who conceived that way and their children are delightful, but it wasn't something I could imagine doing myself.

That left the possibility of asking an acquaintance or friend if he could envisage being the father of my child. But was that really what I wanted? Did I want a man in my life as well as my girlfriend and the child? Did I want to bring up a child with two other people—or even four, if the father had a boyfriend? A family of three seemed to me demanding enough—how would I cope with a family of four or five? Would it mean having to be in a kind of relationship with my child's father?

A few of my gay friends had already asked whether I didn't want a child with them. I didn't. Most of my heterosexual girlfriends thought I'd made a seriously stupid decision when they saw the good-looking gay men I'd turned down: 'What a waste of genes.'

I asked myself whether there was a friend I'd be happy to have about me as the father of my child—someone I liked and loved so much that I could imagine him as part of my extended family. There was only one—but he said no. I think I'd have said no if I'd been him. It would have meant untold consequences for his own life, his own (heterosexual) relationship, his own desire to start a family at some point. The question was indiscreet, impossible, maybe even an imposition, and I understood when he immediately refused.

For a while I let the matter rest. I didn't like the path my thoughts were taking. The whole business made me feel strange—like being on a wife hunt, except that in my case it was a dad hunt. After a while, though, my intuitions became more precise. I'd prefer it if the father lived a long way away, so that he could get to know the child if he wanted, but wouldn't be sitting in our kitchen every evening joining in the debates about whether or not to vaccinate and whether you really need Latin these days.

So I thought of all my male friends, straight and gay, and asked myself if I could imagine any of them as my child's father. What I was really asking was: what kind of a child would I have with them and would I like what they'd be passing on? Once I'd got as far as admitting to myself that the question for me was what my child would get from the man, it was quite straightforward. I imme-diately knew I wanted a child with an American friend of mine. This friend is sensual and athletic, loves eating and reading, and everyone in his family—he, his parents, his brothers and sisters—are generous and genuinely happy.

What could be nicer than if he were to pass something of that on to my child—to our child?

On my next trip to the USA I went to see him and asked what he thought. After thinking it over for a short time he said yes. He made one condition that I found acceptable. And so I flew home happy and relieved. In the years since, the desire hasn't returned. I suspect it's getting too late. But it consoles me to know that I could have done it—that I have a friend with whom I could have had a child.

—

When I ponder the fact that I sometimes see myself primarily as homosexual, sometimes as much more—that although I can feel right and comfortable being part of a 'we', there are times when I long for an 'I'—this well-known image comes to mind, and the discussion about what it is:[55]

'A rabbit's head' is one possible answer. Looking at the picture for the first time, I might see only a long-eared rabbit, facing right—and in that case I'd say: 'It's a rabbit' or: 'It's a picture of a rabbit' or: 'I see a rabbit'.

Why do I think of this? Although it's possible to see what is unmistakably a rabbit's head in the picture, somebody else could claim, and rightly so, to see what is unmistakably a duck's head.

A duck facing left, its beak slightly open. 'It's a duck', 'It's a picture of a duck' or 'I see a duck' would be equally valid answers. Wittgenstein, who discussed the famous duck-rabbit image in his *Philosophical Investigations*,[56] pointed out that if he were seeing it for the first time he wouldn't say: 'Now it's a rabbit'. Convinced beyond doubt of what he saw, he would simply report his perception: 'It's a picture of a rabbit.'

What happens when having first seen only a rabbit (or only a duck), I suddenly become aware of the ambiguity of the duck-rabbit's head? My perception flips and shifts. The ears suddenly become a beak, or vice versa; I see the picture now as a rabbit facing right, now as a duck facing left. The animal seems to flash and change, different each time. Both are 'in' the picture.

There isn't 'more rabbit' or 'more duck' in the picture; the objective qualities of the image haven't changed, only my *way of seeing*. I was sure the image on the picture was a rabbit (or a duck) and had got used to seeing it as such, but now I am seeing differently. Now I now see *aspects* of the picture—situational, variable aspects; I have discovered a new way of perceiving.

Looking for other aspects and figures in familiar images is far from easy. It takes a lot to distance yourself from your habitual way of seeing and search for another way of looking. Tests have revealed that children shown the duck-rabbit on Easter Sunday tend to see a rabbit's head in it, whereas children who are shown the picture in October are more likely to see a duck's head.[57]

We look at images and pictures and get so used to seeing 'fathers', 'Catholics' or 'homosexuals' in them, that we can see nothing else. We nail them down and ourselves with them: 'they're fathers…Catholics…homosexuals'.

As with the duck-rabbit, we see individual elements that confirm us in our judgment. We see parts of a body, clothes, gestures, practices and statements, and we use them to corroborate our perception, to reinforce our judgment: 'That's a woman', 'that's a Jew', 'that's a transvestite'.

It doesn't matter whether they objectively are or not; what matters is the way we look. We see a man in a feather boa and think: 'transvestite'; two women pass us hand-in-hand and we see 'a lesbian couple'. It all seems incontrovertible. But the question is: what if we shift our point of view and look for other figures in the figures that we see?

What happens then?

What happens if we look for the potential father in the man with the feather boa, the potential violinists in the lesbian couple, the potential rugby player in the man with the kippa, the potential lover in the man on the dole, the happy little girl in the child with Down syndrome?

Even if we continue to see a transvestite or a lesbian couple or a Jewish man, we will nevertheless see them differently because, as Wittgenstein would say, not only our description of them has changed but also our visual experience. The Jewish rugby player seems different from the man we could only see as a Jew; the lesbian chamber musicians suddenly seem less one-dimensional and the transvestite, perhaps, now appears to us as mother and father at once.

For anyone who has had to struggle to be seen, for anyone who has had to fight a long political and legal battle for recognition, it's a triumph to be seen at all. But is it enough? Is the resulting situation satisfactory? Is this the way I want to live? Do I really want to have to keep insisting: 'I'm a rabbit, I'm a rabbit, I want you to perceive me as a rabbit'? Don't I sometimes want to be seen as something else as well?[58] I may not be an anteater, but I'm not always just a rabbit.

Sometimes I wish it were possible for us to see *other* people in one another and in the people we meet and talk to—for us to see what *else* we can spot in them, what *else* they might be besides the people we take them for when we first set eyes on them. Sometimes I long for that—long to be able to say: Yes, I am lesbian or gay. Yes, you're right to see me in that way—but it's only one way of looking at me. It isn't wrong; it's true and I recognise myself in the description, but it's only one interpretation. You'd find plenty of other things in the picture too, if you were only willing to look with an open mind—to see me as something else as well.

—

When I'd almost stopped seeing Daniel and he seemed already to have disappeared into another world, he suddenly vanished altogether. We were planning what we'd do when we left school and home and all that had previously held us—and it was then, just as we were on the point of breaking free, that Daniel took his life.

I don't know the how or the why. I was already too far away from him. Later I heard that he'd been seen with another man. Later. When it was too late. When it was no longer possible to find out what it meant—whether he'd been happy again, whether he'd loved, whether...

There are long truths and short truths.

I don't know the truth about Daniel. I don't even know the truth about myself. This story is made up of knowledge and ignorance, of an intuition that has been long in coming and slow to form, that can only be interpreted and reinterpreted—a story told along my lack of knowledge, as if along a crumbling ridge. It can't be true; it can at best be truthful. I know too little because I knew too little back then—about myself, my desire and the square-shouldered boy who sat next to me.

———

I became gay. I still say 'gay', perhaps because it sounds so incongruous—not quite the right word, as if I'd switched 'my' label for another, like in a Shakespearean identity mix-up or one of those Baroque operas where the only character to find his beloved is the one who steals someone else's clothes—or perhaps because the feeling of belonging and yet not belonging is to me the most real. Perhaps because the Front, that dark, rather seedy gay club where everyone could be a foreigner, is still, more than anywhere else, my natural home. Perhaps because people are always thrown by the word and make it clear to me they think I ought to say 'lesbian'.

Perhaps, too, because I still haven't worked out what such a term is supposed to tell us. I don't mean as a political metaphor; that makes sense to me. I understand that we need such terms as linguistic vehicles in political debate—that they increase visibility. Of course I go to Christopher Street Day as a lesbian, and support all demonstrations concerned with the political and social rights of lesbians and gays. As long as homosexuals are still flogged and executed in Iran and Saudi Arabia, as long as homosexuals are attacked on the streets of Poland and Hungary, as long as the Catholic Church speaks in exalted terms of human dignity and human rights, but describes homosexual marriage as 'legalising evil'—as long as all that is going on, I will certainly continue to belong; I will continue to defend such terms.

But over and above that? What does it mean to me, this desire? What difference does it make?

When I think about the way I desire, everything conceptual, everything collective breaks down into single, irretrievable moments, just as it does with everyone else. If I were to try to explain what goes to make my desire, I'd have to describe each one of those moments—how I courted and seduced and fell in love, how I walked home beside her for the first time that winter's night, the snow crunching underfoot, my hands out of my pockets in spite of the cold, so that her hand could brush mine by chance, and how it kept on and on snowing and I wanted to keep on and on walking beside her. I'd have to describe how I opened the door to her that first time in Berlin when she'd supposedly only come to cook, her bag full of fresh rosemary and chanterelles—how she ended up staying, how she stood beside me the first time, sideways on, and I spouted nonsense about universalism, talking and talking, just so that she'd stay there next to me and not go away, so that I could breathe in her smell, so that

I could breathe—and how once, in an exhibition, we couldn't wait and withdrew behind the partition walls to have sex as the other visitors continued to stream past. I'd have to describe that night after 9/11 when we gave vent to all our worries about each other, all our desire, old and new—describe the images of wet, sweaty, bloody, smeary, crumpled sheets, the smell of sex and perfume, the taste of salty oranges and tequila. Like everyone else's, my desire is a whole string of moments: lying, exhausted, in a bed level with the window sill and looking out over her wet back into the white landscape before falling asleep—listening to the knocking of the heating pipes next to the bed in New York. Objects play a part too, each with its own story—that ugly trouser press that was always in the way, the beautiful wooden crate from the other side of the ocean, where the tablecloths were kept—and music, always tied up with one memory or another—Haydn's trio sonatas or the Dixie Chicks. Like everyone else's, my desire knows passionate and dramatic moments, full of lust or delirium, but also moments of heartache and despair, quarrels, tearful goodbyes on the street or at the airport, anger and failure, lies and disappointments—lived, fragile, changeable loving.

Desiring the way I do—and this is *not* the same for everyone else—also means being stared at on the street because we kiss or hold hands, being stared at in a hotel restaurant in the morning because it's clear we've spent the night together—that we've had sex, that we're in love. The looks are sometimes surprised, sometimes hostile, sometimes envious of a happiness that is so urgent and plain to see that it doesn't shrink from being stared at. Some people even venture a timid comment: 'You make a beautiful couple' or: 'I've never seen such a happy pair.'

It also means rarely seeing film characters who love the way we do. It means rarely being able to decide for ourselves when we want to be seen as a 'we' and when as an 'I'—when our otherness matters and when it can be forgotten. It means rarely reading novels where our desire isn't an issue, but something as ordinary and everyday as it seems to us.

It also means knowing who you want to have with you when you wake up from an operation, who is to be family to you in the absence of relatives, knowing when a friend with HIV needs help. It means knowing who'll drive me to casualty if I have to go—preferably someone who expects the same of me, who knows that we're a many-branched tree, a different kind of family, not before the law, but before each other.

And if punishment doesn't swiftly follow,
you must live away your guilt through life.

It also means knowing that I'm not to blame for Daniel's death, that the pain that has accompanied me all these years is a mark not of guilt, but of grief—like my shame at not finding a language back then to say what others should have said. It means knowing that suffering is individual rather than social, that desire has nothing to do with guilt or innocence—that it's only the stories told about desire that try to convince us of that. It means knowing that the only way to hold out against such curtailed, contorted, mendacious stories is to live away the imagined guilt through life—a life full of desire and lust, a life happier than anyone would ever have thought me capable of. And that the only way of assuaging my grief at that past failure to speak out is to write this story—Daniel's story, my story, the story of all those who still suffer today from the silence about desire.

—

ENDNOTES

1   Willibald Gluck, *Orfeo ed Euridice*: http://www.opera-guide.
ch/opera.php?vilang=de&id=131#libretto

(Translator's note: I have followed the German here rather
than translate the original Italian, which is not explicitly
connected with hope and death.)

2   Giving 'the birds and the bees' talk to children is known as
'enlightenment' in Germany.

3   From Lazarus Goldschmidt's German translation of the
Babylonian Talmud (Nidda V, VII, *Babylonischer Talmud*, Vol.
12, Nidda V, VII, Frankfurt am Main, 1996, p. 500), with
reference to the Soncino English translation: http://juchre.
org/talmud/niddah/niddah3.htm#chap05

4   Martin Dannecker and Reimut Reiche, *Der gewöhnliche
Homosexuelle: Eine soziologische Untersuchung über männliche
Homosexuelle in der BRD* (Frankfurt am Main, 1974).

5   See also Jürgen Dehmers' deeply shocking report on sexual
abuse at Odenwald School, *Wie laut soll ich denn noch schreien?
Die Odenwaldschule und der sexuelle Missbrauch* (Reinbek,
2011).

6   From Johann Wolfgang von Goethe's poem *The Erl King*, set
to music by Franz Schubert.

7   Cf. Erwin In Het Panhuis' wonderful book *Aufklärung und
Aufregung—50 Jahre Schwule und Lesben in der BRAVO*

(Berlin, 2010), which has been an important source of research and analysis to me in the following pages.

8   Ibid., p. 62.

9   Ibid., p. 52.

10   Ibid., p. 50.

11   Ibid., p. 38.

12   It is only since the creation of Facebook that there has been a virtual space where young people can express themselves freely, where they can speak a private language in public—a language that says 'I', a language that develops a subjectivity that is otherwise denied them. That didn't yet exist at the time of our first meeting with Ibrahim.

13   The theological grounds for the rejection of homosexuality in Muslim countries are by no means uncontroversial. In his impressive study *Homosexuality in Islam: Critical Reflection on Gay, Lesbian, and Transgender Muslims* (Oxford, 2010), Scott Siraj al-Haqq Kugle argues that there are no verses in the Quran that unequivocally condemn homosexuals and even some that suggest they might be tolerated.

14   Ralf Dose, 'Der § 175 in der Bundesrepublik Deutschland', in the exhibition catalogue *Die Geschichte des § 175—Strafrecht gegen Homosexuelle* (Berlin, 1990), pp. 122–145. See also Rainer Hoffschildt, '140 000 Verurteilungen nach § 175', in *Denunziert, verfolgt, ermordet: Homosexuelle Männer und Frauen in der NS-Zeit*, ed. Fachverband Homosexualität und Geschichte (Hamburg, 2002).

15 Cf. especially the phraseology used by lawyers such as Dr Rudolf Klare, quoted in Hans Georg Stümke and Rudi Finkler, *Rosa Winkel, Rosa Listen—Homosexuelle und 'gesundes Volksempfinden' von Auschwitz bis heute* (Hamburg, 1981), pp. 222–3 and p. 344.

16 On the paranoid fear of contagion in the US army, see also Judith Butler, *Excitable Speech: A Politics of the Performative* (New York, 1997), pp. 103–126.

17 Hans-Georg Stümke, *Homosexuelle in Deutschland: Eine politische Geschichte* (Munich, 1989), pp. 183–4.

18 Ron Steinke, 'Ein Mann, der mit einem anderen Mann...: Kurze Geschichte des § 175 in der Bundesrepublik', *Forum Recht*, No. 2, 2005, pp. 60–63.

19 On the various discussions concerning the 'age of consent' see Ralf Dose, 'Der § 175' (see note 14), pp. 134–5.

20 Interestingly, when the GDR introduced its own criminal code in 1968, Article 151 prohibited both men and women from committing homosexual acts with minors.

21 Ralf Dose, 'Der § 175' (see note 14), p. 123.

22 Ibid., p. 126.

23 In a 1964 interview with Günter Gaus: '"What Remains? The Language Remains": A Conversation with Günter Gaus', *Essays in Understanding*, ed. Jerome Kohn (New York, 1994), p. 12.

24 See J. S. Bach, *The Well-Tempered Clavier*, Part 1, ed. Ernst

Günter Heinemann, fingering András Schiff, Henle Urtext. See also Siglind Bruhn's intelligent analysis, *J. S. Bachs Wohltemperiertes Klavier: Analyse und Gestaltung* (n.p., 2006).

25 *The Glenn Gould Reader*, ed. Tim Page (New York, 1984), p. 16.

26 Georg Büchner, *Leonce and Lena*, Act I, Scene 3.

27 Joseph Brodsky, *Less Than One: Selected Essays* (New York, 1986), p. 7.

28 Ibid., p. 8.

29 *The Shere Hite Reader: New and Selected Writings on Sex, Globalisation and Private Life* (New York and Toronto, 2006).

30 Cf. Hubert Fichte, *Interviews aus dem Palais d'Amour* etc. (Hamburg, 1972), pp. 5–6.

31 See Lydia Cacho, *Slavery Inc: The Untold Story of International Sex Trafficking* (London, 2012).

32 Cf. *Dokumentation 'Homosexuelle bespitzelt'*, ed. Hamburger Lesben- und Schwulen-Verbund in co-operation with *Du + Ich* (Hamburg, 1980).

33 Cf. Rolf Zundel, 'Der Weg eines Gerüchts', *Die Zeit*, No. 9, 1984: http://www.zeit.de/1984/09/der-weg-eines-geruechts

34 Cf. the title story of the *Spiegel*, No. 3, 1984: 'Kohl: "Das läuft nicht gut"', in: *Berichterstattung des SPIEGEL zum Thema Homosexualität, 1947—August 1990*, ed. Verein zur Förderung der Erforschung der Geschichte der Homosexuellen in Nordrhein-Westfalen e.V. (Cologne, n.d.), p. 294.

35 Cf. 'Ein Abgrund von Sumpf hat sich aufgetan', ibid., p. 305.

36 'Soldaten als potentielle Sexualpartner', ibid., p. 295.

37 Military Counterintelligence Service report by Brigadier Behrendt, ibid., p. 306.

38 Ibid.

39 'Es geht nicht um meine Rehabilitierung', *Spiegel* interview with Kiessling, ibid., p. 293.

40 I have written at greater length on the matter of dealing with 'false' or pejorative allegations in *Kollektive Identitäten— soziophilosophische Grundlagen* (Frankfurt am Main, 2000/2010), p. 121.

41 The potential impact of such allegations on the internet is demonstrated by the case of Joel, a boy who took his life after being exposed to sexual defamation on the web. See Rebecca Casati, 'Geh sterben, Du Schlampe', *Süddeutsche Zeitung*, 9/10 April 2011, weekend supplement. Such cases are complex: on the one hand, they describe the very real humiliation of young people or adults who are called 'gay' and see it as social defamation; on the other hand, such defamation would have no effect if the allegation of 'homosexuality', whether true or false, weren't branded as problematic.

42 Ludwig Börne, '74. Brief aus Paris vom 7. Februar 1832', *Briefe aus Paris*, ed. Manfred Schneider (Stuttgart, 1977), p. 146.

43 For a critique of one-dimensional identity politics see also Amartya Sen, *Identity and Violence: The Illusion of Destiny* (London, 2007).

44 A laudable exception is Maren Kroymann, an actor who is trusted by directors to play almost any role, regardless of her private preferences.

45 Translator's note: In German, these notes spell Shostakovich's initials: D-Es-C-H = D(mitri) SCH(ostakovitsch).

46 See the astute analysis of the representation of AIDS by Brigitte Weinart, *Ansteckende Wörter, Repräsentationen von Aids* (Frankfurt am Main, 2002), pp. 7–8.

47 'Eine Epidemie, die erst beginnt,' *Der Spiegel*, No. 18/1983, p. 147.

48 'Ich bin en Tunt, bin Kernjesund', *Der Spiegel*, No. 29/1984, p. 134.

49 Quoted in an article by Robert Pears, 'Health Chief Calls AIDS Battle "No. 1 Priority"', *New York Times*, 25 May 1983.

50 'Ich bin en Tunt' (see note 50), p. 133.

51 See the information on the adoption rights of lesbians and gays provided by the Lesbian and Gay Association of Germany: http://www.lsvd.de/recht/ratgeber/adoption/adoption.html, or the material on the 'legal status of homosexual parents' compiled by the Federal Agency for Civic Education: http://www.bpb.de/themen/BXH32F.html

52 Since the initial publication of this book, the laws in Germany have changed. From 1 October 2017, marriage is no longer restricted to being between a man and a woman: https://www.bundesrat.de/SharedDocs/texte/17/20170628-ehe-fuer-alle.html

53 The 'Sample Guidelines on the Implementation of Assisted Reproduction', issued by the board of the German Medical Association on the recommendation of the German Advisory Council, states: 'In view of the child's wellbeing, methods of assisted reproduction must, on principle, be used only by married couples.' (http://web.archive.org/web/20120510002108/http://www.bundesaerztekammer.de/downloads/kuenstbefrucht_pdf.pdf)

54 In a statement on the German Medical Association's guidelines, Manfred Bruns, the speaker of the Lesbian and Gay Association in Germany, argues that the comments on the guidelines are 'non-binding interpretations'. He stresses the need to interpret them constitutionally, in which case lesbian couples couldn't be banned from using assisted reproduction any more than heterosexual couples. As is clear from the authorisation rule (§13, section 1), the 'guidelines on assisted reproduction' are to prevent the unethical behaviour of doctors when carrying out artificial insemination. The artificial insemination of civil partners is no more unethical than that of married couples—or of couples in a consensual union, who are also permitted the use of donor sperm by the guidelines. https://www.lsvd.de/recht/ratgeber/adoption/adoption.html

55 The 'Kaninchen und Ente' ('Rabbit and Duck') figure first appeared in the German magazine *Fliegende Blätter* on 23 October 1892 and was subsequently used by the psychologist Joseph Jastrow in his book *Fact and Fable in Psychology* (Boston, 1900).

56 Ludwig von Wittgenstein, *Philosophical Investigations*, translated by G. E. M. Anscombe, third edition (Oxford, 1968), pp. 194 seq.

57 P. Brugger and S. Brugger, 'The Easter Bunny in October: Is it Disguised as a Duck?', *Perceptual Motor Skills* 76, 1993, pp. 577–8.

58 The American author Daniel Mendelsohn describes how a similar longing or intuition was communicated to him through the structure of ancient Greek: the 'both-and', the *men* and the *de*, 'on the one hand' and 'on the other', opposites that aren't exclusive, that can exist at one and the same time: 'If you spend a long enough time reading Greek literature, that rhythm begins to structure your thinking about other things too. The world *men* you were born into; the world *de* you choose to inhabit.' *The Elusive Embrace: Desire and the Riddle of Identity* (New York, 1999), p. 26.